T

MARRIAGE AND FAMILY

And How to Have a Happy Marriage

IS SUBMITTED
IN PARTIAL FULFILLMENT
OF THE REQUIREMENTS FOR
THE

DOCTORATE OF CHRISTIAN EDUCATION

INTERNATIONAL APOSTOLIC UNIVERSITY

MAY 31, 2002

AUTHOR: Oce Jones

Copyright © 2006 by Oce Jones

How to Have a Happy Marriage
by Oce Jones

Printed in the United States of America

ISBN-13: 978-1-60034-614-9
ISBN-10: 1-60034-614-6

All rights reserved solely by the author. The author guarantees all contents are original and do not infringe upon the legal rights of any other person or work. No part of this book may be reproduced in any form without the permission of the author. The views expressed in this book are not necessarily those of the publisher.

Unless otherwise indicated, Bible quotations are taken from the King James Version of the Bible.

www.xulonpress.com

Contents

Preface vii
Dedication ix
Acknowledgment xi
Abstract xiii
Introduction xv

1	Communication	47
2	Conflict	59
3	Listening	69
4	Destroying Myths	77
5	Money Management	83
6	Spiritual Guidance	89
7	Trust/Honesty/Expectations	103
8	Quality Time	111
9	In-Laws/Extended Family and Friends	115
10	Intimacy	121
11	Identifying Strengths and Weaknesses	129

Conclusion 145

Bibliography 153

About the Author 155

Preface

This project was formed with husbands and wives in mind; couples who desire and are willing to improve, build and progress towards healthier, happier and more joyful marriages. It gives me tremendous joy to realize that the information presented in this book will be instrumental in building bridges to deeper love and more meaningful and successful relationships.

How to get your needs met, your desires fulfilled and improve the quality of communication between each other, reconcile/resolve conflict, increase your sensitivity to each other's approach and increase your abilities to listen to each other is the primary focus of this work. Discovering and establishing a solid foundation for your relationship is our goal for you. Become aware and explore new spiritual dimensions and heights in your relationship.

A creative learning experience and a positive journey towards a healthier, happier relationship is what this project strives to deliver.

Dedication 献星(の辞)

I dedicate this project to help those who love and desire to be loved. That you will experience and enjoy happy, healthy and prosperous marriages is my wish and prayer for you.

I am deeply indebted to my wife, Mattie who is also my best friend. For your love, patience, prayers, unselfish support and a wonderful marriage throughout the years, thank you.

I recognize our children Natalie, Valerie, Kimberly, Oce Jr., and Vincent, who have enriched our lives immensely. Included in this dedication are loving memories of our son, Charles, whom we miss dearly.

Finally, to my daughter-in-law, Noreen, I convey a very special thank you for the loyal support you provided in preparing this project for publication

Acknowledgments

I thank God, my Lord and Savior, Jesus Christ for providing me with the inspiration, guidance, wisdom, knowledge and strength to bring to completion a project of this magnitude. For providing me with the organizational skills to systematically address the godly principles that make marriage a workable institution, how can I pay the debt of gratitude?

Also I acknowledge and thank my wife Mattie Jones for her support of this project. The tireless encouragement you provided throughout the formation of this project is gratefully acknowledged.

Abstract

Any marriage can work, as long as both individuals are willing to do what it takes to make it work. Love and a successful marriage require hard work. My goal is to provide you with the skills, insight and the knowledge necessary to create, build and maintain strong, healthy and lasting relationships.

The tools given to you will include invaluable shared experiences and relevant facts about men and women as they relate to the institution of marriage. You will become aware of and learn behaviors that have the power to restore your marriage. Practices that build happiness and love will be provided. Suggestions will be provided to you and your partner on clear, concise, and effective strategies to survive marriage's challenging and difficult times so that your union will last. The approach will be effective communication, conflict resolution, compromising, and learning to be a good listener. Love is usually why we decide to get married; yet most of us are not equipped to fulfill this, our strongest desire. This will be your guide to "The Good Marriage."

Introduction

Marriage and the family, traditionally, have been held sacred. Divorce rates are soaring, but you can have a happy and loving marriage. Changes in family and the household composition are a part of every individual's life. From childhood throughout adulthood, we accumulate life experiences. Until the day we die, our lives continue to develop and evolve.

There is no secret to a long healthy, happy and strong marriage. A good marriage is the result of not just work, but hard work! Building a strong, lasting and happy marriage is serious business that involves working hard, consistently. Strains and challenges are inevitable in all marriages, but with wisdom and spiritual guidance, a strong marriage can be established. Husbands and wives must equip themselves with love, understanding, trust and an honest commitment to meet the challenges and pressures of marriage and family.

Life changes deeply impact our views of marriage, family and happiness. Using real-life experiences, forty years of marriage, and my experience as a marriage counselor, let's concentrate on the essential steps that every marriage must take to overcome the difficulties that arise in all relationships. Carefully applying these steps will put your marriage on a solid footing.

Husbands and wives gain strength from spiritual guidance. Communication, compromise, listening, destroying myths, honesty and a determination to have a successful marriage and family – all of these are critical elements necessary to build a strong, successful marriage.

The type of information that will be covered here is designed to help husbands and wives better understand each other.

We will examine myths that society encourages and many misguided notions. You will discover alternative methods while discovering approaches that work best for your individual marriage.

By the time we reach adulthood, we think we know who we are and the type of mate we want to marry. Our views have been formed based on observations, what our parents have told us to look for in mates and what we have idealized as the picture perfect, ideal mate. Often our expectations that have been set are unrealistic, preconceived notions.

A lack of communication in any relationship leads to destruction and a breakdown in intimacy. According to Statistical Abstract of the United States 120th Edition, *The National Data Book,* (2000), since 1975 statistical data shows that the rate of divorce has increased to an astounding fifty percent.

How to Have a Happy Marriage

I have found that men respond to what they see; whereas, women react to what they feel. Women often feel that men do not listen and are more concerned with sex. Women want intimacy, and want to know "why can't men listen". We must destroy the myths and create love. Love is an equally shared responsibility.

If you think that you know everything there is to know about marriage and relationships, then think again! According to statistical data reported by Acock and Demo, (1994, p. 149), there are as many divorced individuals as there are married couples.

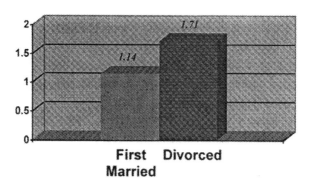

Another study conducted by Robins and Regier, 1991, is as follows:

Married (never divorced)	1.5
Divorce once	4.1
Divorced twice	5.8

How to Have a Happy Marriage

What you don't know could hurt you! Whether you have been married forever or are newly wed, what you do not know can hurt you. In a marriage, failure to nurture and deepen your love, commitment, or union, could very well ignite a fuse that is capable of eventually exploding, resulting in the breaking up of your home, your family, and your heart.

Long-lasting and affectionate marriages are never "ending". They will progress in one of two ways; 1) continuously grow or 2) become stagnate.

My wife, Mattie, and I have been married for almost forty-years, but we continue to dramatically improve our love through the practices that you will learn through this research. When I discover something that strengthens the quality and improves my marriage, I share it and spread it with our church congregation and as many other husbands and wives as I possibly can.

I am excited about the platform this book gives me to share my experiences, knowledge and findings with other couples. You will discover invaluable strategies and facts concerning how to develop, nurture and cultivate a wholesome, lasting marriage.

When I discover techniques that can be instrumental in reconciling marriages that have experienced turmoil or have gone astray, I cannot keep these techniques to myself. I feel compelled to help couples find their way back to experiencing love, happiness and contentment.

As a pastor, marriage counseling is one of my responsibilities. In an effort to rejuvenate and revive marriages after the husband and wife have tried everything they know, I introduce them to workable solutions that will help to rekindle their motivation to rebuild their marriage.

Many couples meet, fall in love and ride off into the sunset. Many couples find themselves madly in love and anxious for marriage; not realizing that it takes more than just an emotion to make a marriage work. The average number of years that marriages last, in America, is five to seven years before becoming victimized by divorce.

The average person feels that a good marriage will work if they love each other, are committed and stay involved for a lifetime. Many couples feel that these are the pre-requisites that determine how well they will "get along".

Being in love is an important factor and one of the keys to a successful marriage; however, marriage involves and requires more skills than simply loving or be in love with each other. In a marriage you must know how to argue and resolve conflict and effectively nurture the needs of your spouse. Conflict, when handled properly can induce positive changes in a marriage.

As a marriage counselor, my experiences, subject to my hearing, on a regular basis, to many never ending marriage stories. Usually one of the spouses does not share what they were feeling for fear of hurting the other's feelings. Therefore, everything seemed fine to the partner, which is misleading, because over time a lot of negative emotions have festered. For instance, following is an example given by Parrott III and Parrott, 1996, (pp.71-72)

My wife says I never express my feelings, and I say she has enough emotions for the both of us. We genuinely want to understand each other, but often get tangled up in the different ways we each express our feelings.

Too often in marriage we take for granted that our spouse should know exactly how we are feeling. But that's unfair. Feelings are too fickle and unpredictable to put that burden on another person. Listed are strategies that can help you express feelings in a way that will allow your spouse to truly understand them.

1. Be careful not to place blame. Rather than making the statement *"You make me furious."* or *"You are driving me crazy;* , say *"I'm furious." Essentially, these same statements can be* rephrased by simply taking responsibility for them. Instead of saying *"you make me furious, just say* , *"I'm furious." Instead of blaming each other for your anger, simply state how you feel by saying, "I feel confused and crazy."*

2. Be honest. It is tempting to describe dinner with your in-laws as *"fine or very pleasant,"* when actually, the whole evening, you were bored and irritated. It is easier to say that *you're tired and just want to go to bed* when actually you are worried about the finances and afraid to bring up the subject. Though temptation to skirt around the real issues may be difficult to resist, failure to express your true feelings creates an atmosphere where it is harder to genuinely express the true emotions that you are feeling.

3. Be congruent. It can be very confusing when your tone of voice and body language is not consistent with your words. If you say *"I'm not angry"* while

How to Have a Happy Marriage

your tight face communicates a message contrary to what you are saying, what should your partner believe; your words or your nonverbal behavior?

If your spouse wants and needs more available time for her and the kids, she should clearly express her desire. Communicate your needs to your companion. In many cases, couples wait until things are intensified and on the verge of driving them apart physically and emotionally.

Accordingly, Parrott III and Parrott, (p.76) supports the fact that, in every cell of our bodies, women and men differ. For example, a woman's blood contains fewer red cells, causing them to tire more easily.

In the literature review of *Questions Couples Ask*, Parrott III and Parrott, (p. 76-77) a question was asked about gender: *I hear a lot of talk about how men and women have different needs, and I am the first to admit it's true., I acknowledge, however, I have a tough time trying to pinpoint these needs so that I can better understand my wife and I think she feels the same way about me.*

Many marital problems evolve because men try to meet needs that they would value and women do the same. The problem is that since the needs of men and women are often so different, we waste effort trying to meet the wrong needs. Since men and women have very different needs, we must strive to understand these differences. Learning to appreciate our partner's differences and becoming committed to meeting those unique needs is crucial to the strength and harmony of marriage.

How to Have a Happy Marriage

Willard F. Harley, in his popular book *His Need, Her Needs*, has given us a great tool to do just that. He identifies the most important marital needs of husbands and wives. You may or may not agree with all of them, but they can serve as a good discussion starter:

She needs affection. It symbolizes security, protection, comfort, and approval. A hug expresses affection. And for the typical wife, there can hardly be enough of them.

He needs sexual fulfillment. Just as women crave affection, men want sex. And they don't just want their wives to make their bodies available. They need to feel their wife is as invested in sex as they are.

She needs conversation. Not just talk about her husband's problems or achievements, but about her problems and her hopes. She needs quality conversation on a daily basis.

She needs honesty and openness. Mistrust destroys a woman's marital security. If a husband does not keep up honest communication with his wife, he eventually undermines her trust and destroys any hope of security.

He needs an attractive spouse. A man does not need a super model for a wife, but he wants her to make an effort to be attractive to him. He wants her to dress in clothes he likes and in a style that is appealing to him.

She needs financial support. A husband's failure to provide sufficient income sends shudders through the underpinnings of a marriage. A woman needs to know that her husband is taking care of their family's needs and their future.

He needs domestic support. Old-fashioned or not, most men fantasize about a loving, pleasant home where few hassles occur and life runs smoothly.

She needs family commitment. Wives want their husbands to take a strong role in the marriage and express how important it is to them. They need to see evidence of a strong commitment to family life that is not over shadowed by work or anything else.

He needs admiration. Honest admiration is a great motivator for most men. When a woman tells her husband (who has been sweating it out at work) that she thinks he's wonderful, that inspires him and keeps him going.

As stated before, you may not agree with all of these "needs," but they are worth seriously considering. Discuss how each of your needs differ and the plan of action you will employ to meet those needs.

Many couples neglect rejuvenating their marriage by not learning or adding something new to their relationship. The information I am sharing will not only broaden the thought processes of couples, but it will radically change lives and improve the quality of marriages. It will open the doorway to new ways to obtain the ultimate relationship.

The expectation of what a marriage offers has evolved from earlier generations. Years ago, a marriage offered the chance to have children and the opportunity to build a home and grow old together. Having children is important because it is God's way of replenishing the earth and keeping the generations going, Genesis 9:1. Genesis 30:1, implies that if a woman was childless she was cursed or did not have the favor of God. For Rachel said to her husband "give *me children or else I die.*"

Over the past twenty years, husbands and wives expected to enjoy a wider range of benefits ranging from producing families, financial security, friendship, housework, home repairs and sexual pleasure. Is it really more difficult today than it used to be to maintain a successful, happy, long lasting intimate relationship? If you were to base your answer on the divorce rate, the answer would be yes. Husbands and wives must be willing to do what is required to accomplish these high achievements.

This literature shows that when husbands and wives use the different sources of information presented to them in this book, regarding marriage, both before and during marriage, divorce rates decline significantly. Visualize the remarkable reality of couples staying together with their children for thirty and forty years. It is possible for children to grow up in loving and stable homes! The change would be monumental, and would impact our society in a very positive way. Crime rates would decline. The sky rocketing number of many teen pregnancies would become significantly less. Drug and alcohol abuse would become nearly non-existent. Spousal and family abuse, and many other social problems could be resolved or eradicated.

When two parents are actively present in the home, the degree of stability and certainty in a child's life is greater. In an environment tempered with love and affection; harmony and a strong sense of identity and belonging is more easily is established. Specifically,

How to Have a Happy Marriage

David Blaukenhorn:1990 wrote, *more than 36 percent of all children in the nation were living apart from their fathers-more than double the rate in 1960.* The trend shows no sign of slowing down. Indeed, it seems quite probable that as of 1994, 40 percent of all children in the nation live apart from their fathers. It is a fact that we teach our children with more than our words. Children are tremendously impacted by the actions of their parents. Without the guidance of parents, in the home, the chance of a family becoming dysfunctional increases tremendously. In fact, sixty percent of all children in black communities are represented by absentee fathers. Black children are being raised without black father figures in the home. Studies show that 82% of all black children born in the ghetto are born out of wedlock. Ninety percent of children in ghetto schools come from broken homes and they are reared by their mothers, grandmothers, or themselves. Not only is the pregnancy rate among black females higher than that of any other race, but more crack babies are born to black females. (Jerry Buckner, Religious Broadcasting/February 1995.)

The future of your marriage is up to the both of you. Only you can determine your level of happiness. While the possibilities are endless; the choice is yours. In your pursuit of the skills and techniques that will enable you to stay happily married, you will obtain what it takes to maintain a true and lasting intimate marriage. If it seems simple; concentrate on the fact that while communication, compromise and listening may come naturally, these skills must be developed and honed. Doing so will empower you to

How to Have a Happy Marriage

achieve a higher level of success and satisfaction in your marriage.

Men and women are essentially different. This is one reason that we must take these skills to a higher level. The dynamics of two radically different individuals trying to fit each other's style and mindset can be complex. Women and men are known to have different definitions for the same word. Take for instance the word *"intimacy"*. To a man, intimacy usually means that they are "doing" activities with someone. A woman's version of intimacy is expressed by "sharing" verbally about her experiences. When these two genders, in marriage, are placed in the same house, the result is usually two people honestly trying their best to interpret the needs of their spouse, based on their interpretation or definition of what they think their spouses' needs are. Within the environment of marriage, an awkward, sometimes painful, and more often than not, frustrating situation can be created. If the couple does not seek help, before long, the two can be driven into a situation that typically leads them to divorce. Often this happens without the individuals even realizing or understanding how their relationship progressed to this critical point of frustration. Typically, both individuals will wonder or ask? *What happened*?

It is imperative that men and women learn to understand the differences in their needs to fulfill emotional intimacy. Bridge those differences through learning effective communication, compromise and listening skills. Differences in conflicts and lack of compromise between men and women can lead to

How to Have a Happy Marriage

an unsatisfying and frustrating marriage. Women are sometimes too harsh and critical of their spouses. Men can be too distant, too independent, accusing their wives of trying to control and being the head of household. Men may take the approach of lecturing when trying to solve a problem, while a woman's only purpose is to be understood and heard. The observation of the researcher: 90% of our problems come from the lack of understanding. In the book of Proverbs, Chapter 4; verse 7, it says *"and with all thy getting get understanding."*

Developing meaningful communication, compromise, resolving conflict and listening is the core of a loving marriage. These elements are crucial to a relationship and oftentimes couples do not know how to get there with their mate. However, communication is the beginning point, upon which a successful marriage is built. Effective communication will take a marriage to the desired destination. Compromise requires both parties to come together at a mid-point where conflict subsides and listening, understanding and displaying compassion enhances love.

You can banish the most common divorce patterns from your relations and turn your conflicts into opportunities to develop a better love. There is no question that communication is a key factor to the success and satisfaction in a relationship. Why? Communication is the tool necessary for developing and understanding the needs of the other person. Proverbs 25:, verse 11 says: *A word fitly spoken is like apples spoken pertinently, in proper time and place."* Instructions, advice, comfort encouragement

How to Have a Happy Marriage

and affirmation give seasonably. To create an environment to communicate is to take time to understand. Set aside time everyday for you and your spouse to communicate. Take turns sharing the event of your day. Have each partner concentrate on what the other is saying. Acknowledge what you hear and validate the other person's feelings. Remember that there is no wrong. What is important however, to you, may be different from what is important to your partner. Communication is more than verbalizing and hearing the words of someone speak. Good communication takes place when someone hears what you are saying, understands what you mean and validates what you are feeling.

Life is full of experiences, and it is those experiences that give us knowledge and understanding about life and how to apply what we have learned for our success in life. I often wonder why the more important aspects of life were not taught in school such as: husband and wife relationship, money management, insurance, child training and other relevant issues which life consists of. The divorce courts, filed bankruptcies, rampant lack of respect, and lack of self-control that children so openly display in today's society is blatant evidence that the essentials of life are not being taught.

The livelihood and well being of our society is based upon the roots and foundation of marriage and family. The church has been defined as one of the safe havens. The church, therefore, should seek to teach and prepare society for the seriousness and responsibility of marriage. Based on the Apostolic

xxviii

doctrine, within the church lies the power to restore the ethics, values and morals necessary to rebuild family structure.

According to Jerry Buckner, Religious Broadcasting, Black Males an Endangered Species: February 1995, "Religious Broadcasters in America focus on issues which are pertinent to society, and perhaps none is so urgent as the plight of black Americans. The issues involved, although volatile in nature, can be handled by religious broadcasters with honesty and sensitivity. It is time for these issues to be addressed because time is running out. Whatever problems that occur in the suburbs of white America or in white communities cannot compare with those afflicting the black community. Black males are an endangered species."

After forty years of marriage, my wife and I have remained bonded and loyal to each other. We are firmly committed to our marriage and have made our love for each other a priority. In the early years of our marriage we had to learn how to adjust to each other and this was a time when patience had to be demonstrated. Every marriage has its ups and downs, but when two people love each other and have made a conscious commitment to stay married, they will survive the difficult times. If they agree to uphold the vows of "unto death parts" then a foundation has been established that they can build upon.

My wife and I have established this foundation, and have made the choice to remain together, no matter what the obstacle. With this attitude we have built a strong, solid, loving, happy relationship, that has lasted forty years.

This is not to say that we did not have disagreements, misunderstandings and some tears, but we have learned how to communicate with each other, and resolve issues without unnecessary havoc. It is sometimes difficult to determine whether you should communicate all of your concerns to your companion. Choosing not to communicate or misinterpreting the communication is one of the primary bases of many marital problems. Once there was a situation where I needed to talk to my wife about a serious and sensitive issue. I pondered for three days, trying to find the right words to say, and the right time to speak. When the time and opportunity presented itself to speak to her, we were able to work the situation out, without problems or complications. When talking out problems with your spouse, it can be hard to sit there and be quiet, especially when you feel the other is wrong. However, learn to listen until the other stops speaking before you give your input. Try not to disagree with everything that is said. Show that you respect your mate by waiting until he/she is done speaking, before tossing in a rebuttal. As a loving and caring spouse, your response should show your willingness to work things out, Proverbs 15; verses 1-4 says: *A soft answer turneth away wrath: but grievous words stir up anger. The tongue of the wise useth knowledge aright: but the mouth of fools poureth out foolishness. The eyes of the Lord are in every place, beholding the evil and the good. A wholesome tongue is a tree of life: but perverseness therein is a breach in the spirit.*

Learn to view each conversation as a gift. You have learned of issues that could have otherwise been kept inside and possibly caused difficulty if the problem had not been aired. Once communication has taken place; this gives your companion an opportunity to address the issue. Couples must learn to listen, wait their turn to speak and more importantly hear what their spouse is saying and try to understand the rationale behind what their spouse is saying.

Every marriage is a journey. Each level should take you closer toward the desires of the heart. Effective communication, compromise, and listening are basic skills that bring about a long lasting and satisfying marriage. When a man and a woman are able to put aside their pride and defensive armor they are able to open their ears to each other and come to concession. Now they are able to move forward toward the ideal marriage. I have taken my forty years of experience in marriage and this research based on couples to use as a tool to improve marriages.

Great marriages require work. Most of us are willing to work hard at satisfying our spouses, but in many cases we need help in understanding what it is we are working toward. We need to set up an institution of premarital classes and training in churches, and other institutions that perform marriages, such as the justice of the peace, and ordained ministers. These efforts will serve as a counterattack on the high rates of divorce and the rising statistics of unhappy marriages.

It is time to do something about the all-too-frequent divorces. Scripturally, from the beginning, divorce was never permitted. Matthew Chapter 19, verses 8-9 says: "*He saith unto them, Moses because of the hardness of your hearts suffered you to put away your wives: but from the beginning it was not so. And I say unto you, whosoever shall put away his wife, except it be for fornication, and shall marry another, committeth adultery: and whoso marrieth her which is put away doth commit adultery.* People have a right to learn a better way to live and to know how to deal with unhappiness and inner discontentment prevalent in so many marriages. The church must educate and implement training programs that include tests that prepare prospective spouses for the inevitable challenges of marriage. Based on the Apostolic doctrine, the word pertaining to marriage must be spread. The church should develop and teach preparation for marriage from a spiritual aspect. Developing more programs designed and geared towards strategically facing the challenges of marriage and decreasing the divorce rates should become a high priority among spiritual leaders. Based on doctrinal truths, I would like to see the church become more adamant about placing emphasis on the truth: If one abides by the word and commandments of God, their marriage has a higher rate for success. Supporting scriptures from the Apostolic doctrine: Song of Solomon, Chapter 1, verse 2; *Let him kiss me with the kisses of his mouth: for thy love is better than wine.* Ephesians Chapter 5: verses 1-2; *Be ye therefore followers of God, as dear children; And walk in love, as Christ also hath loved*

How to Have a Happy Marriage

us, and hath given himself for us an offering and a sacrifice to God for a sweet smelling savior.

Romans, Chapter 7, verses 1-3; *Know ye not, brethren, (for I speak to them that know the law,) how that the law hath dominion over a man as long as he liveth? For the woman which hath an husband is bound by the law to her husband so long as he liveth; but if the husband be dead, she is loosed from the law of her husband. So then if, while her husband liveth, she be married to another man, she shall be called an adulteress: but if her husband be dead, she is free from the law; so that she is no adulteress, though she be married to another man.* Doctrinal truths applied to marriage relationships decrease the divorce rates.

Dr. David Olson, pre- and post marriage evaluation exam with 195 questions is said to be the best test for predicting the outcome of marriage before the wedding day.

Real people, real situation: My husband Tony (not his real name) is the chairman of the youth department of the church we attend. His position requires him to be involved in the youth activities. On this particular occasion, a summer trip to Columbus, Ohio was planned for a youth retreat. I found out about the trip through the grapevine, a casual conversation with members of the group. The youth members were discussing all of the details, the date, time of departure, hotel reservations, and the activities.

Not only did hearing this information surprise me, it was coming from everyone other than my husband and that made me very angry! How could it be that others knew of his plan, yet he had not shared

xxxiii

How to Have a Happy Marriage

any information with me? I sleep next to him at night and live in the same house, but my spouse had not mentioned a single word to me. Not only did this trip cause me to be angry, it also caused conflict because I was left for the weekend with our two-year-old and without a means of transportation. I was upset that he did not consider me when making his plans, nor did he find me important enough to communicate with me prior to making a final commitment. I began to wonder if he cared at all about my feelings, or if he was aware of the problems that are created each time we do not communicate on such matters.

Married couples should communicate with each other so that they can prevent conflict. Couples should consider their spouses when making plans, no matter how small the activity. An activity that appears to be meaningless or small to one individual, may be extremely important to the another. Practicing mutual respect helps to avoid unnecessary conflict. Effective communication is the key element to successful relationships. Communication of one's thoughts, feelings, and emotions can strengthen a relationship. Effective communication gives clear insight to the needs of an individual; rather than the other partner having to guess or try to figure out what is going on inside of their companion's heart and mind. Clear communication makes it possible to cater to feelings of disappointment or a feeling of loneliness when emotions are verbally expressed. Emotions that are held secretly and are causing unhappiness have a less likely chance of being fixed when held inside and not shared with the other person involved in the marriage.

xxxiv

How to Have a Happy Marriage

From a man's prospective, according to Gary Smalley, 1979, "Many of the problems couples experience are based on one simple fact. Men and women are TOTALLY different. The differences emotionally, mentally, and physically are so extreme that if a husband and wife don't put forth a concentrated effort to gain a realistic understanding of each other, it is nearly impossible for them to have a happy marriage" (p.28). Individuals should share what is going on within, so that the spouse has the opportunity to fix and make things better. Couples should not assume that their companion automatically knows what they are feeling, if that individual has not communicated what their emotional needs are.

The woman is more concerned than the man with keeping the family structure together. For example, Smalley argues that "Women tend to be more "personal" than men. Women have a deeper interest in people and feelings, while men tend to be more preoccupied with practicalities that can be understood through logical deduction."

Dr. Cecil Osborne says that women tend to become 'an intimate part" of the people they know and the things that surround them; they enter into a kind of "oneness" with their surroundings. A man relates to people and situations, but he usually doesn't allow his identity to become entwined with them. He somehow remains apart. That's why a woman, viewing her house as an extension of herself, can become easily hurt when it is criticized by others.

By nature the women are more nurturing; therefore giving her more experience in nourishing, and taking

xxxv

How to Have a Happy Marriage

care of the needs of others. It is not what you can get out of the marriage, but what you can put into the relationship that matters. Both partners must contribute to the marriage, for the well being of the family.

Husbands and wives must relearn some of the traditions, and mannerisms they have been taught by parents, grandparents and other sources of influence. Not all family traditions and behaviors are acceptable once you're married. These things may have negative bearings on a marriage. For example, the wives from the older generations were taught that their husband should not see them naked. Women were taught to be ladies in the bedroom; therefore, not to show any signs of enjoyment during sex. There were other fables such as, too much sex is not healthy, or women are not to be aggressive in the bedroom. She should not approach her husband and ask him to be intimate with her.

These are examples of morals and principles that are taught by families and passed down from generation to generation. These ideas may not necessarily prove to be beneficial to the marriage. Couples, however, must do what is best for their individual marriages. Make adjustments according to the needs of your spouse, which may differ from traditional values you have learned. Biblical teachings such as Song of Solomon deals with the pure love, mystical union and marriage of Christ and his church. In the New Testament, the union of Christ and the church brings out this understanding. Matthew 22: verse 2 says: *The kingdom of heaven is like unto a certain king, which made a marriage for his son.* Revelation

19, verses 7-9 says: *Let us be glad and rejoice, and give honour to him: for the marriage of the Lamb is come, and his wife hath made herself ready. And to her was granted that she should be arrayed in fine linen, clean and white: for the fine linen is the righteousness of saints. And he saith unto me, Write, Blessed are they which are called unto marriage supper of the Lamb. And he saith unto me, These are the true sayings of God.* Revelation 21:2, And I John saw the *holy city, new Jerusalem, coming down from God out of heaven, prepared as a bride adorned for her husband.* II Corinthians 11; verse 2, says: *For I am jealous over you with godly jealousy: for I have espoused you to one husband, that I may present you as a chaste virgin to Christ.*

It is often said that opposites attract. I am not in total agreement with this fallacy. Couples should have things in common. It is also important to be able to compliment each other with an offset. When one companion is weak in an area, the other should be strong and vice versa, to offset the given situation.

I am grateful to God for my wife. She knows how to diplomatically work situations out with our children. She is a wealth of knowledge, has insight and knows how to rectify issues in ways that I am unable to.

Showing love and concern, is an outward emotion that should be expressed. As a child, I do not remember my parents saying, "I love you" to each other. Nor do I recall them telling my siblings, or myself that they loved us. It is possible that they did, and I never heard it. On the other hand I am not sure that I ever told my parents them that I loved

How to Have a Happy Marriage

them. However, I have learned from experiences that expressing love outwardly through deeds and actions is important to all relationships. My wife has made it known to me, that I can never say, *"I love you"* to her too many times. If two or three days have passed and I have not uttered the words "I love you", she reminds me to do so. When you say, "I love you" enough, it becomes automatic in making it into an action word. Love is an action word. I became creative in different ways to express "I love you" to my wife. How many different ways could I show her that I love her? My wife says she feels that we have a perfect marriage, and I agree with her.

There are couples that expect too much from a marriage. They feel that love just happens. They feel that there should be no disagreements, no misunderstandings, no hurt or pain. If that is the path that a marriage has taken, then someone is not being realistic; nor, are they in a marriage. Taking the passive approach does not make for a healthy marriage.

Marriage isn't necessarily for everyone. There are individuals who choose not to marry. The Bible teaches that Paul made the choice not to marry. If one makes that choice, the Bible says that they are better off so that they can be more faithful in the service of the Lord. Additionally, if one chooses not to marry, as stated in 1 Corinthians 7: verses1-2; *Now concerning the things whereof ye wrote unto me: it is good for a man not to touch a woman. Nevertheless, to avoid fornication, let every man have his own wife, and let every woman have her own husband.*

How to Have a Happy Marriage

For those contemplating marriage, weigh out the pros and cons. If the good out weighs the bad, then you may want to move forward with your plans. On the other hand, if the bad out weighs the good, back up and give marriage a second thought. Apply the same concept to existing marriages. If there are more pluses than minuses, continue to work things out and strive for longevity. One of the problems of marriages today is that, couples do not give the relationship enough time to mature and develop into a good, long lasting, and loving marriage. It takes time to build a good relationship. It could range from two to ten years to adjust, before a relationship becomes stable and strong enough to survive crisis situations. The secret to surviving crises is that, although initially viewed as a negative situation it can develop and strengthen a marriage.

During a crisis, do not make decisions or choices when you are acting on intense emotions. Your decision would be based on how you feel at that very moment. Usually when a person is angry, they are prone to act irrational, and do not use sound judgment. When the dust settles and your emotions are under control, you will be more rational when making decisions.

Years ago, I found my three-month-old daughter in the bed dead. This was a crisis for us, but we shared the pain and sorrow that we were both experiencing. It was important for the both of us not to place the blame on either of us. We searched for answers but were not able to find any. We merely had to accept the fact that, it was our time to experience crisis. Until the occurrence of an actual crisis, it is typical

xxxix

How to Have a Happy Marriage

for us to think of ourselves as being exempt from real crises. Incidents like this only happens to other people is a common thought process. This time, it happened to us. It was a time to support, encourage and to affirm each another. Romans 8 verse 28 says: *and we know that all things work together for the good to them that love God, to them who are called according to His purpose.*

I recently taught a Bible class on marriages. The subject was focused on spouses setting their minds and purposing in their hearts, to love their companion, regardless of the situation or circumstances prevailing in the marriage. Loving your spouse, in spite of what your spouse does, or does not do is a very selfless act. This is a great stepping-stone and advantage against arising problems and an example of obeying God, according to 1 Peter 3 verses 8-9: *Finally, be ye all of one mind, having compassion one of another, love as brethren, be pitiful, be courteous: Not rendering evil for evil, or railing for railing: but contrariwise blessing; knowing that ye are there unto called, that ye should inherit a blessing.* To paraphrase, let all be harmonious, sympathetic, brotherly, kindhearted, and humble in spirit; not returning evil for evil, or insult for insult, but giving a blessing. When a spouse purposes in their heart, to love their mate regardless of the problem, they have chosen to allow love to be a determining factor, not anger, pride or stubbornness.

Romans 7, verse 3: as supporting scripture, *So then if, while her husband liveth, she be married to another man, she shall be called an adulteress: but if her husband be dead, she is free from that law; so*

xl

How to Have a Happy Marriage

that she is no adulteress, though she be married to another man. There are no contingencies to this statement. The man is to love his wife. God is not a one-sided God. He also said in Ephesians 5:22-24, *For the husband is the head of the wife, even as Christ is the head of the church: and he is the saviour of the body. Therefore as the church is subject unto Christ, so let the wives be to their own husbands in every thing.* When each party does what God requires, every element for a successful marriage is waiting for us, if we only seek God first, Matthew 6: verse 33, *But see ye first the kingdom of God, and his righteousness; and all these things shall be added unto you.*

The average person responds according to how they are treated. If we are treated well, the response is positive. When treated badly, the response is negative. If a marriage is developed according to God's word, a response cannot be based on treatment.

Most men are conditioned by society to believe that they are naturally capable with all the leadership qualities and women should play an inferior role at home in personal affairs. They also mix the same values of male superiority. In the book of Ephesians 5, verse 23, *For the husband is the head of the wife, even as Christ is the head of the church: and he the saviour of the body.*

The Bible says that husbands are the heads of the wives, even as Christ is the head of the church; therefore, it is his responsibility to create and maintain a spirit of love, unity and peace in the home. The welfare, support and happiness of the home, becomes the responsibility of the man.

xli

As the husband, I feel that it is my job to take care of my wife and my children. I do not want someone other than myself taking care of my responsibilities. We may not have everything that we desire to have; nor do we eat at the finest restaurants. I provide what I can; therefore, we must learn to be satisfied and content with what we have. More importantly, be thankful.

I read an article that said, "Unhappy marriages can harm your health." Democrate and Chronicle 2000, March. The article also argued that, a happy marriage might protect women from strokes and heart attacks, after menopause. The article continues with, "a miserable match also makes its mark, as can be seen on ultrasound scans of aorta and arteries. Scientists have reported that this puts women at a higher risk for dying of cardiovascular diseases." Therefore, this argument concludes that having a happy marriage works like a good medicine. There is no merit in being married for a number of years and not experience happiness. There was another article about a couple that was married for seventy-one years. They attributed their success to being friends and enjoying each other's company. The couple made the statement; "Understand what's important to each other and do not take each other for granted".4

Once couples accept and realize the responsibilities of marriage, they will understand that they must, (1st Corinthians chapter 7 verse 3) "Render that which is due to each other". Your time is no longer yours to do what satisfies you. You must render affection, kindness and respect. By nature, the average person is selfish and is only concerned with pleasing himself or herself. Marriage means that two people have made the decision to join together and function as one. Here is how making a commitment to marriage should be viewed.

You know that there is much more involved in making a marriage, but you have proved that you are ready to begin this new adventure. Most feel that they have what it takes to make a marriage work. God designed the marriage covenant as a special commitment between man and a woman so that no other relationship would take priority over this promise. Marriage is the responsibility of both spouses to have moral obligations to God and each other to protect their relationship from someone or something.

Satisfied with your knowledge, the preacher smiles. He's now ready to lead you in the vows that will join your lives and officially send you on your journey. But before your lips may come together in the wedding kiss, your minds must be forever entwined; you will become the unit of constantly friction-free agreement, as promising to always work together for the good of the relationship instead of an individual agenda.

"Are you ready to be joined with one another, to become a unit of "We", instead of a "Me?" the preachers asks. "I know from what you have told me that you realize that the word "we" means you are a team, a permanent combination of who you both are in sharing what is best for the both of you. Now that you have begun this journey toward marriage, you may no longer demand your own way, but a way that is best for the marriage. Everything that you do from this moment on will affect the marriage. Are

xliii

How to Have a Happy Marriage

you ready to proceed?" You nod your heads in agreement and the preacher continues.

Please repeat these vows after me and in the spirit of future communication between the two of you, do not let it linger on your lips. Do not repeat these vows and then forget them, but instead allow them to permeate your being and your life. For these are the laws that you must live by; their denial, neglect or invalidation will immediately send you back to where you began, and you will have to start the journey over again, perhaps even alone. And then the preacher begins reciting your vows. "When there are difference and conflicts between you, which are normal, do you promise to take turns and carefully listen to each other?"; he asks.

You smile at each other and say in unison, "We do". Do you promise to set you own opinions, concerns and expectations aside during your conversation and do all that you can to understand what your mate is saying and understand who he or she is as a person?" "We do." you say. "Do you promise to accept and value your mate's uniqueness as separate from you but also special and treasured?", he asks.

The point being made is marriage is a serious commitment. Promise yourselves that you will not succumb to conflict, division or waste away.

It takes courage to do special things for your spouse when the majority is setting the example of doing nothing for their companion. In marriage, it is okay to sweat the small things, especially when it pertains to opening the car door for her first, and pulling out the chair at the dinner table. It always

xliv

adds sweetness to the marriage when you call each other by pet names.

Love is a decision. "*Love is that which causes one person to desire the most good to come to another and is willing to do whatever is necessary to bring it about*". (Rev C.W. Blast)

For a marriage to last, couples should spend quality time together. Love is spelled T.I.M.E. When two people decide to get married, they are making a statement that "I want to spend all of my time with you, in fact, I want to spend the rest of my life with you." According to the New Hite report, titled Women and Love, 90% of divorces are initiated by women and not men. Women spoke of how they just like spending time with their husbands, whether it was vacationing, or working in the yard or going to dinner, cooking together, lying-in in bed reading or even in conversation. Another writes, "The best part of being married is the companionship and being together," another form of the physical warmth and comfort. It is not wise to become so grossly involved in your hobbies, social events and community activities, etc., to the point that it takes quality away from your spouse. We live in such a fast pace society that, if one does not take the time to spend with their spouse, it will eventually have a negative affect on the marriage. It is absolutely necessary for couples to get away from it all and be together alone.

Couples should spend quality time together so they do not drift apart. If couples do not spend

How to Have a Happy Marriage

quality time together, they increase the risk of taking each other for granted and drift apart. When couples spend quality time together, it gives them an opportunity to relive those special moments; the special moments that caused them to fall in love. Couples should acknowledge the good qualities in their mates and express their appreciation. Spending quiet quality time allows couples to get closer, to develop a oneness and to reminisce. Spending quality time allows time to develop an emotional intimacy.

Now, let us begin the steps to how to have a successful, happy, and loving marriage. Remember, it will take hard work, courage and concentration to achieve this goal, but once you have experienced love to this degree, you will never want to settle for "lets just stay together for the sake of the kids". You can experience true and lasting love in your marriage.

Chapter 1

Communication

Chapter One

Communication

Communication is the most important vehicle for a marriage. Understanding just how essential communication is will help you to bond in your marriage. Husbands and wives, please realize the incredible power of words. Proverbs 18: verses 20-21 says*: A man's belly shall be satisfied with the fruit of his mouth, and with increase of his lips shall he be filled. Death and life are in the power of the tongue: and they that love it shall eat the fruit thereof.* Words have the power to hurt, heal, tear down or build up. Make it a practice to use words that encourage, strengthen and heal.

How do you define the word communication? What form of communication do you practice in your marriage? Woolfolk writes, "*Communication is more than just verbalization and hearing the words someone speaks. Good communication takes place when someone:*

How to Have a Happy Marriage

- *Hears what you are saying*
- *Understands what you mean*
- *Validates what you are feeling*" (p. 58).

There are many forms of communication, including verbal, non-verbal, body language, tone of voice, facial expression, and even a sigh. Positive communication creates an environment of affirmation. Smalley writes *"The climax of all communication in marriage is the special time we share in intimate discussion. While a lot of communication and many conversations are essential in marriage, the highlights of marital communication are the special times of deeply personal, intimate conversation.*

As you establish a protective atmosphere in which open communication can flow, you should cherish and seek special times to share your innermost thoughts, feelings, and dreams. In these intimate times, share with your spouse the deep, positive expressions of your heart about how much you love him or her.

"This may occur as you two sit alone in a special moment, or even in the afterglow of sex, but do not take these special times for granted. And do not hide your inner self from your spouse. The more you open up, becoming honest and vulnerable, the more you truly will know each other, and the deeper your intimacy and love for one another will be."

When a person believes that they are valued, respected and appreciated, they express positive behavior and attributes to building a strong and healthy marriage. "Non-verbal communica-

How to Have a Happy Marriage

tion, such as body language and facial expression, make up 55 percent of the total message. Tone of voice, including sighs, makes up 38 percent of the total message. Nonverbal behavior is vague and primarily expresses attitudes." According to Adler and Elmhorst (1999), "Even after first impressions have been made, the impact of nonverbal behavior is powerful. In fact, when nonverbal behavior seems to contradict a verbal message, the spoken words carry less weight than the nonverbal cues. The claim that nonverbal cues carry more impact than words might seem preposterous. Consider as an example how facial, bodily, and vocal behavior could shape the meaning of a statement such as, "Thanks a lot for your ideas. I'll think about them." The same words could convey sincere appreciation, indifference and dismissal, or sarcasm and anger. This example shows the critical role that nonverbal communication plays in conveying meaning".

"Social scientists have discovered that men and women typically use speech for different purposes and in different ways. Female language emphasizes rapport and the creation and maintenance of relationships to a greater degree than male speech which is focused more on the "report" function of communication: accomplishing the task at hand and asserting control over the situation" (Adler and Elmhorst, 1999) (pp. 96,97). Language can sometimes communicate and generate undesirable feelings, therefore when communicating with your spouse, be sensitive to their emotions, needs and reactions.

How to Have a Happy Marriage

Also, spoken communication does not necessarily convey the real message. For example, your mate senses there is something bothering you. She asks you what's wrong. You mutter, Nothing, "as you slam the cabinet door", Woolfolk, (p. 58). How well you communicate your feelings makes the difference in the success or failure of your relationship. Learn to express yourself clearly to reduce the likelihood of pitfalls and misunderstandings. Clarity in communication is essential to a healthy marriage.

There is a story of a man whose job transferred him out of the country. His friends thought that he would surely be unfaithful to his wife, since he was far away for an extensive period of time. The young man had his heart and mind set differently then that of his friends. This man kept the communication going between him and his wife. He wrote her letters constantly, faithfully on a weekly basis. He also called as frequently as he needed to keep his focus on her. He told her how much he missed her, and how he could not wait to be with her again. Because he maintained constant communication as a result, the young man never strayed away. He was able to remain faithful to his wife until he returned to her.

In another situation, Eric and Elaine (not their real names) have been married for five years. Eric finds his way to my office because he wants to leave his wife and wants a divorce. He no longer wants to be married, because there are characteristics about his wife he does not like. There were issues of not enough sex, she goes to bed too early, and she talks too much. Eric was able to communicate his concerns to me

How to Have a Happy Marriage

about his companion, but had neglected to express his concerns with the individual involved. I ask the question, have you told your wife how you feel. His response was "no". How can his wife fix the problems, if she does not know what the problems are?

Reggie Jackson said it best: *"You work to make a successful marriage. It isn't just enough to be the breadwinner and for your wife to be a caring and supportive helpmate. You have to talk: husband to wife, man to woman, human being to human being."* A lack of communication or misinterpretation in communication is one of the major leading causes for marital problems. Do not just communicate, but aim for honesty. Partners should not pretend to go along with the program just to keep the peace. Open, honest, clear and effective communication does not mean cruelty. Whatever you have to say, can be said without hurting, or causing your partner to feel unloved. One should not begin statements with "if you really loved me." It is unreasonable to expect your companion to know what you want, without you telling them. Spouses are not psychics.

Timing is everything. When there are issues to be discussed make sure you approach your companion at the right time. For example if she is working full time, attending college full time and overwhelmed with additional obligations, perhaps you should wait to tell her that the house is in disarray and looks untidy. Likewise with the wife, if your husband is basking in the event of the basketball championship, that would be an inappropriate time to expect his undivided attention to ask him to assist with chores.

How to Have a Happy Marriage

Genuine communication begins with the most direct way to tell your partner that you are concerned and want to hear of his or her feelings and needs. Communication is vital to any marriage and is a way of sharing our needs. It is the key to the deepest closeness and understanding of your mate. Honest communication is our opportunity to show our mates who we are. Couples should talk, talk, talk and talk. Do not allow anything to build up and fester inside. In relationships, you are not going to agree on everything, but show respect for what the other thinks and feels. Make sure that you listen to your mate, even when a problem is the topic of discussion. Do not avoid listening because a problem exists. We try to fix what we have preconceived, through non-verbal communication, a saddened facial expression or a difference in body language, rather than pay attention to what our mate is saying. The growth and success of a marriage depends on the quality of communication.

Woolfolk suggests that, "In business, poor communication can lead to disaster and financial failure. In international affairs, it can lead to war. In personal relationships, poor communication can lead to partners becoming stranger and the eventual breakup of the relationship. There are literally millions of unhappy couples that don't make an attempt to see the world from each other's point of view. Love is a union of two different people who must continually make adjustments in order to maintain an affectionate relationship." (p. 56)

Couples should not get caught up in the stereotypical training that "communication is conflict."

How to Have a Happy Marriage

Couples should not run from communication, but learn how to embrace it and treat as a viewpoint that will enhance their lives. It takes two to communicate; a speaker and a listener. To be a good communicator you must learn to play both roles, listen then speak when it is your turn.

Accordingly, Evans confirms, "Words possess incredible power, power to wound or heal, to destroy or buildup. We must discipline ourselves to use words that build up, strengthen, encourage, and heal. The opposite occurs with our spouses because of frustrations or hurts. When you realize you have launched verbal missiles, repent and ask for forgiveness."

Communication is essential to bonding your marriage. It does not matter how long you have been in the marriage or how good your marriage is; otherwise, you cannot become close as a couple without good, effective, healthy communication. There are cases where couples have been married for over ten years or more and still do not know each other and continue to be distant in their relationship. Just because you share a house, children, bedroom, checkbook or many other things if you do not share your thoughts and feelings through open communication, nothing else matters. Open, honest, clear, effective communication is the most important element for our marriage relationships to grow and build a durable foundation.

According to Evans, "Good communication in a marriage can occur only when the needs and differences of each spouse are understood and respected." For example, for a man to communicate properly to his wife, he must understand her need for deep, detailed communication. A woman does not want headline answers; she needs the details, the full story.

When a man does not understand a woman's need for patient, detailed information, he will often resent her need to know. In fact, many men believe their wives are interrogating them or mistrust them because of their desire for information. Instead, men must understand that God created women with this need. Just as husbands must understand their wives, wives you must also realize the needs of her husband.

The strength and intimacy of the marriage relationship is fully dependent upon both spouses' willingness to freely communicate. Your wife's need for open communication is as important to her as is your need for sex. To turn off the flow of your words to her has the same impact upon her as when your sexual needs are turned off.

Men must learn to accept and appreciate how important their words are to their wives. From early in the morning until late in the evening, day in and day out, the words we speak to our wives create the world they must live in. If this is a safe, loving world of abundant provision, our wives will flourish and respond to us accordingly. However, if this atmosphere is harsh and unfulfilling, we must realize the danger this environment produces for our wives and, consequently, our relationships with them.

Also just as men must understand and accept the differences in their wives, there also are some differences wives must understand and accept in their husbands. Men are emotionally different from women. How and where they communicate is different. Men

How to Have a Happy Marriage

are emotionally modest and physically immodest. Although a man doesn't mind revealing his body as much as a woman, he is much more careful about uncovering his soul.

Women are the opposite. A woman is physically modest and emotionally immodest. She is much more self-conscious about her body, and about where and how she reveals it. The same woman who is so modest about her body will stand at the checkout counter and tell a perfect stranger some of the more intimate details of her life. It can be quite amazing to a man to hear a group of women talk. Although women see such conversations as healthy and normal, it is quite uncomfortable and unnatural for most men.

Because a woman is physically modest, she needs a protected atmosphere to be able to enjoy sex, a safe and protected environment to be able to open up and share her body. But most men can enjoy sex almost anywhere, no matter who is round.

In this same way, because men are emotionally modest, they need a protected environment in which to open up emotionally and begin to talk. Men are frustrated and violated when they are expected to "spill their guts" with other people around or when they have just walked in the door from work.

Ladies, if you are in the habit of telling family and friends everything that goes on in your marriage and/ or all the things your husband says and does, don't expect your husband to open up. Men are frightened and violated to think their wives betray them by sharing the details of their lives with someone else.

How to Have a Happy Marriage

While it is appropriate to share certain things about your life and marriage, you must carefully communicate to your husband that he can trust you. Remember, if you violate his emotional modesty and safety, it has the same effect as if he showed his buddies at work naked pictures of you and explained the details of your sex life.

To summarize, we all need to realize the incredible power of our words. We must also understand it is impossible to build a strong marriage without regular, healthy communication flowing in both directions. Finally, we need to remember in communicating how our spouses are different and how to accommodate these differences (Evans, pp.215-217). Matthew 12, verses 36-37 says: *But I say unto you, That every idle word that men shall speak, they shall give account thereof in the day of judgment. For by thy word thou shalt be justified, and by thy words thou shalt be condemned.*

Chapter 2

Conflict and Anger

Chapter Two

Conflict and Anger

According to Parrot III and Parrot, anger and marriage go together. The reason given is because of the amount of time spent together. It creates more opportunity for anger to erupt. We also let our guard down with ones we love more than we do with others. This creates opportunity not only for more intimacy but also for more frustration and anger. Although conflict and anger becomes par for the course with most marriages, anger certainly should not be given free license to dwell as it please. Conflict and anger without limits can lead to terrible destruction. Conflict must be controlled. However, there are principles in which couples can learn to deal with this inevitable feeling that holds such potential destruction. (1996)

Learning to resolve conflict should be mandatory training for marriage. Ephesians 4; verses 26-29 says: *Be ye angry, and sin not;: let not the sun go down upon your wrath: Neither give place to the devil. Let him that stole steal no more: but rather let him labour, working with his hands the thing which is good, that he may have to give to him that needeth. Let no corrupt communication proceed out of your mouth, but that which is good to the use of edifying, that it may minister grace unto the hearers.* The way conflict and anger are handled will determine whether a marriage survives. Harsh words lead to broken trust and hurt feelings. Hostilities that are held within kill romance. In order to survive the conflicts of married life, couples must learn to reconcile. Do not take the normal response to being hurt, misunderstood. It is neither okay nor healthy to strike back and to get even.

In successful marriages, one should not develop an attitude of let me out of here when conflict arises. Conflict avoidance is not the answer to the problem. Couples should not deal with conflict by looking for an escape route. Some individuals go shopping, but the problem is still there when they return. Others drink alcohol, some become workaholics and others turn to drugs, and there are others that pack up and abandon the relationship. The problem does not get resolved until you deal with it.

Couples should trade in the spirit of "getting even" in exchange for the spirit of resolution. Scripture tells us that we were created to live in harmony and communion with others. We were created for peace. 1 Timothy 2; verses 1 - 2 says: *Exhort therefore, that, first of all, supplications, prayers, intercessions, and giving of thanks, be made for all men; For kings, and for all that are in authority; that we may lead a quiet and peaceable life in all godliness and honesty.* When

How to Have a Happy Marriage

a spirit of rebellion dominates in a marriage, every little conflict escalates into harsh accusation. When marriages take on the spirit of resolving reconciliation, major conflicts can be discussed and worked through.

The Bible tells of a wealthy tax collector that ripped people off without remorse, until he had a heart-to-heart encounter with Jesus Christ over an unscheduled dinner. After the meal and brief conversation, this unsympathetic extortionist surfaced from his house a changed man. With trembling lips he begged for forgiveness of those he had taken advantage of and cheated, and promised to repay them four times over. He even vowed to give half of all his future earnings to the underprivileged. It is not enough for one spouse to be willing to resolve conflict or have a spirit of reconciliation. Both must be willing to work through situations peacefully. Both must lay down their weapons, admit their wrongs and mistakes and find a way to work through to a solution.

Seek God for a spirit of reconciliation. Establishing peace with him is the most important step you can take, for both you and your marriage. For those that marry out of the faith are equally yoked together. If peradventure God will grant a good marriage. For those who marry in the faith are to be reconciled according to 1 Corinthians 7; verses 10-11 says: *and unto the married I command, yet not I, but the Lord, Let not the wife depart from her husband. But and if she depart, let her remain unmarried, or be reconciled to her husband: and let not the husband put away his wife.* Matthew 5 verses 23-24, says:

Therefore if thou bring thy gift to the altar; and there rememberest that thy brother hath ought against thee; Leave there thy gift before the altar, and go thy way; first be reconciled to thy brother, and then come and offer thy gift.

Conflict is often viewed as an unfortunate situation. Resolving conflict effectively is a humbling experience. Becoming defensive or angry, when you and your spouse are faced with conflict or tension is not the answer. Proverbs 15: verses 1,18 says: *A soft answer turneth away wrath; but grievous words stir up anger. A wrathful man stirreth up strife: but he that is slow to anger appeaseth strife.* Proverbs 14: verse 29 says: *He that is slow to wrath is of great understanding: but he that is hasty of spirit exalteth folly.* Ecclesiastes 5: verse 2 says: *Be not rash with thy mouth, and let not thine heart be hasty to utter any thing before God: for God is in heaven and thou upon earth: therefore let thy words be few.* Ecclesiastes 7: verse 9 says: *Be not hasty in thy spirit to be angry: for anger resteth in the bosom of fools.* There are ways that you can use indirect approaches such as control your language, softening your voice, or try listening to fulfill your mate's needs for healthy conflict resolution.

This worked well for my wife and I, but only after we applied what we had learned from previous experience. I like to go fishing, and my wife likes to go shopping. We compromised on the matter and we both came out of the situation happy. I take her shopping before I go fishing. My wife is made content and happy; then after she is done shopping I go fishing for as long as I like. Compromising is definitely a better solution, as opposed to arguing and getting upset over such matters.

A good compromiser should be willing to be a good listener, be able to respect the other person's point of view, and be sure to take a non-confrontational approach. Consequentially, there are times when we may have to lose the battle in order to win the war. Your wife may not agree with the decision, therefore you may simple have to live with the decision. It is not whether or not a person is right or wrong. The important factor is being able to meet each other midway between differences and come to a settlement. Discussing the situation at hand when emotions are flaring is not wise. Words spoken out of anger are very difficult to take back, and can cause emotional scars, Proverbs 6: verse 2 says: *thou art snared with the words of thy mouth, thou art taken with the words of thy mouth.* Proverbs 13, verse 3 says: *He that keepeth his mouth keepeth his life: but he that openeth wide his lips shall have destruction.* Walking away from the matter gives time for the atmosphere to settle. Overcome those natural feelings of stubbornness or feelings to impose authority. Each side must make concessions. Learn how to resolve any conflicts or differences with a solution that is agreeable to both partners. Conflict is inevitable. Situations will occur. There is no escaping them. One of the best ways to deal with conflict is to put yourself in the other persons shoes, and try to relate and understand their position from their point-of-view.

How to Have a Happy Marriage

Wisdom of scripture provides excellent guidance. *"Be angry but do not sin; do not let the sun go down on your anger"* (Ephesians 4:26). In other words God admonished us not to sulk in anger and drag it out a long time. Couples should never go to bed angry. Acknowledge bruised emotions and feelings of pain and find a resolution or compromise. Make it a practice to build your relationship daily so that no problem builds up.

When conflict arises, implement these steps to help build a strong marriage. Treat your marriage like it is more important than any other issues.

- Establish a set time and place for discussion.
- Define the problem clearly.
- Acknowledge your wrong and what you contributed to the problem.
- Walk away from the situation when problem-solving talks become too heated.
- Do not issue threats, personal attacks, or ultimatums.
- Compromise on how each person will work on the solution to the problem.
- If your solution does not work, start over, using the same steps to conflict resolution.

Another important factor to resolving conflict is to focus on solving the problem, not controlling the other person. Control shows a lack of regard for the other person's needs and opinions and it can cause problems in the marriage. The goal is not to solve the problem "my way" or "your way" but rather to develop a resolution that meets everyone's needs. Try

How to Have a Happy Marriage

negotiating a win-win solution. More importantly, alleviate landing any verbal punches and sounding judgmental. Avoid using language that will trigger negative emotions, or defense arousing statements. Avoid beginning statements with the word "you". This type of approach provokes defensiveness. Try to use language like: "I" was not patient with you, during your difficult time. Do not call names or use stirring labels. Instead of attacking the other person, show concern for your mate. If you have caused the indifference, a simple apology will work wonders.

When handling conflicts assertively, one must identify the problem; identify the goal you are seeking, and choose the best time to speak. Think over what you want to say and how you can say it best.

Chapter Three

Listening

Chapter Three

Listening

Listening is vital in a marriage. It can improve the quality and closeness in a marriage, or have the opposite effect when listening is poor. Communication begins with listening. Listening is the basis of respect. Every human being needs and wants to be heard. Why is listening so important to a marriage? Adler and Elmhorst point out one major reason is time: *listening is the most frequent and arguably, the most important type of communication. Studies conducted over 60 year ago indicated that adults spent an average of 29.5 percent of their waking hours listening.*7 These were the results:

     Listening   32.7%   Writing   22.6%
     Speaking   25.8%   Reading   18.8%

Listening is learning how to understand, evaluate and open your mind and ears. Proverbs 4; verse 7 says: *Wisdom is the principal thing; therefore get wisdom: and with all thy getting get understanding.* Listening will give you an opportunity to help your mate solve their problems. Listening to your spouse can save your marriage.

Be sure to state your desires clearly so that your needs will be met precisely. Repeat what you want until your spouse understands you, reassuring that you have clearly communicated your thoughts. You want to be sure that your personal feelings and needs are being heard. It is important to express your needs to your spouse; however, while he is watching his favorite show may not be the time to ask him to listen to what is on your heart. Revisit the situation at a better time. Avoid negative interruptions and focus on the main points. It is easy to assume that you understand your spouse, only to discover later that you were wrong. Learning to repeat what you have heard is a safety check that can reduce and eliminate misunderstandings. Make sure that you understand what has been said.

Furthermore, questioning and paraphrasing can reveal valuable information. Stop talking and learn to listen. There are times when remaining silent and permitting the other person to speak can be beneficial. Rather than making assumption, and being judgmental or probing for information, give your companion time to explain their feelings and points of view. If you are the cause for the hurt and pain your spouse is experiencing, you must take on the role of listening for the duration of the conversation.

Couples should know that it is more important to listen than to talk. Doing something else when your spouse is communicating does not count as listening. Make it a point to practice active listening, which requires attentive behavior. Listen until the other person stops speaking before a response is given, so that the person that is speaking feels that they are being heard. A good listener maintains eye contact and nods of comprehension as points are explained. A good listener shows concern and is not anxious to jump in to give a rebuttal. Couples should listen to each other's situations without passing judgement; nor should a person be made to feel ashamed when confidential information is shared. Withhold judgment and listen first. Take time to listen, make sure that you understand, and then evaluate.

Poor listening skills will incur consequences. Some of the biggest problems created from poor listening comes from inaccurate and unproductive assumptions. Let's face the facts; in a not so perfect world, despite the importance of understanding others, the average person's quality of listening is generally poor. Research suggests that misunderstandings are the rule, rather than the exception. Conversationally, partners typically achieve no more than 25 to 50 percent accuracy in interpreting each other's remarks.[8]

Now that we are aware of listening and communication barriers, why not take action to eliminate listening problems. First let's begin with egocentrism. Your own ideas are not more important or valuable than your spouse's point of view. Be careful not to develop an egocentric attitude. Such an attitude

How to Have a Happy Marriage

not only creates poor listening, it prevents you from hearing and learning important information, which ultimately alienates you from the very person with whom you need to learn how to build a better relationship. Communication depends on the receiver as well. The most well expressed thought is of no use if one's companion fails to listen. The clearest expression will not prevent misunderstandings, if one companion isn't paying attention or thinking about something else. Both partners, the speaker and listener, must share the responsibility of reaching an understanding. Good listening can be hard work.

When a person remains silent, silence should not be taken for passivity. Passive listening is sometimes the best approach to listening, in an effort to stay out of the way and encourage one's companion to speak openly and freely. At first glance, it seems that the person speaking has control, while the listener follows. Western society tends to correlate listening with weakness, passivity, and lack of authority or power.9 In my opinion, listening is equally important as talking. Effective listening is one of the most effective relational devices that can be used to keep in touch with your companion's deepest emotions and desires. In some situations, it is okay to keep quiet to hear what your companion has to say. Developing a genuine desire to understand your mate, and alleviate hurt, frustration, and confusion requires the ability and skill of a good listener. Listening should be used as a relational tool that helps keep interaction between couples running smoothly. The value of learning to listen cannot be emphasized strongly enough.

Listening is an area that should be given high priority in a relationship. For most of us we do not realize the effort and work that becoming a good listener involves. Communication is the number one complaint of most wives and has been determined to be one of the more serious criticism of husbands. Many times when wives are expressing their points of view, disappointments and desires, the conversation falls on deaf ears. In a recent survey conducted by the researcher, the question was asked. "*Doest my partner listen to me when I describe my feelings?*" Forty percent of the respondents agreed, 5% strongly agreed, 15% were neutral, 15% disagreed and 25% strongly disagreed. The results of the data analysis fully supports the hypothesis that partners are not listening.

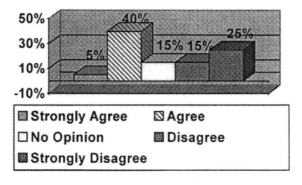

Chapter Four

Destroying Myths

Chapter Four

Destroying Myths

A myth is a story that has been passed down from generation-to-generation based on religious beliefs, people, places or things. Generally myths are accepted as facts. Myths are destroyed by educating ourselves to the facts and truths of the subject. 1 Timothy, chapter 1 and verse 4-7 speaks of fables: "*Neither give heed to fables and endless genealogies, which minister questions, rather than godly edifying which is in faith: so do. But refuse profane and old wives fables, and exercise thyself rather unto godliness.*

Intimacy is an important part of marriage. We all are exposed to influences that have shaped our sexual attitudes, some which can take the pleasure out of a perfectly natural act. Many individuals enter into their marriages believing myths that are harmful and haunt intimacy in the bedroom. Following are examples of myths that can be harmful and produce negative results in marriage:

How to Have a Happy Marriage

- Women have often been told, "Men are dogs." This means that women cannot trust men. Men are believed only to be after sexual conquests, not a loving, caring relationship with a woman.

- Men have told each other that women want to consume them, castrate them, tie them up and imprison them.

- Women are told that it is up to the man to give her an orgasm. They are told that if the man did it right, she would have thrilling sex.

- Both men and women are told that if they do not have an orgasm, they cannot have good sex. .

- Women have been led to believe that to desire or enjoy sex is not ladylike. Their sexual role is to serve men and make them happy.

- Both men and women are told that if their partner really loved them, he or she would know what they like without being told or given direction.

These are only a few of the popular myths commonly accepted as truth. These commonly believed myths cause problems in a marriage and especially in the bedroom. Sex was intended to enhance love. We must free ourselves from myths that stifle and regiment natural pleasures to be enjoyed in the context of marriage.

It is also critical that spouses do not use sex for dominance or punishment. When angry with each other, manipulating the sexual part of the marriage is not the way to solve problems. Problems should be solved before they become too big to handle and certainly before they negatively affect, control or dominate intimacy in the marriage.

Couples should learn to delight themselves in the bedroom. Do not allow the interfering beliefs to deny you the deepest level of intimacy in your relationship. Practice positive sexual habits such as:

Free yourself from the myths that prevent you from appreciating and enjoying your body. Freely give and receive pleasure from your spouse. Express delights with sounds of joy. Communicate with your body. Save the talk for some other time, except love talk.

Be experimental. Push yourself to try something new. Leave shame out of it, but respect the limitations of your mate.

Learn to take your time.

Always remember that you are making love, not having sex. Keep your love making centrally focused.

As to the frequency of intercourse, there should be no shame. Frequency does not make you into anything less of a lady. Find some way to clearly

How to Have a Happy Marriage

communicate your need and readiness to each other. The act of sex does not bind, mend or cure a bad marriage. It does, however, enhance the joy and pleasure of a happy marriage.

Chapter Five

Money Management

Chapter Five

Money Management

If you are losing sleep worrying about your credit or the money you owe, then you know that debt can be a major source of stress in your life. The burden of debt can negatively impact your mental and physical health, marriage and family relationships.

Based on the results of this study, the researcher places great emphasis on money management and personal finance. Financial hardship is the second leading cause to marital problems and divorce. Financial difficulty also leads to stress, as validated by (Kapoor, Dlabay, Hughes:2001).

"Financial planning is designed not to prevent your enjoyment of life but to help systematically, help you obtain the things you want. Too often, however, couples make purchases without considering the financial consequences. Some people shop compulsively, creating financial difficulties. Detailing your living expenses and your other financial obligations in a spending plan will save you from over

How to Have a Happy Marriage

burdening yourself and your marriage from financial stress. Spending less than you earn is the only way to achieve long-term financial security" (p.22). Financial difficulties causes stress. The word stress has many nuances and definitions depending upon the perspective of the individual.

Stress can be described as a loss of control. Stress is considered to be an absence of inner peace or a state of anxiety produced when events and responsibilities exceed one's coping abilities. Stress, when left unresolved can destabilize all aspects of your life.

Diggs and Paster support the claim that when there is not enough money it sometimes causes anxiety and stress in a marriage. Whatever the reason for a lack of money, it can generate feelings of helplessness, anger, and depression. All of these adverse effects can cause a serious blow to the marriage. It takes effort from both partners to hold the relationship together. When there are hard times due to lack of money that is not the time to find fault, or walk away from the marriage. Think of ways to adjust the way that money is being spent. Something must be done to relieve the pressure that could be destroying your marriage. Financial matters have a long history of causing marital friction. It is imperative that you know "who should do what" when it comes to money.

It is a good idea for partners to share equally the responsibilities of budgeting, investing and saving money. When you are dividing up the tasks, consider your individual talents rather than the stereotypical roles, such as the wife doing the laundry, washing the dishes and giving the children a bath. Or the husband

How to Have a Happy Marriage

takes out the garbage, mows the lawn and pays the bills. Bringing home the most money does not make you a financial expert.

Some debts may be more emotionally stressful for one partner than for the other such as child support payments, money owed to family members, and doctor bills. If there is a negative connection for one partner, it may be best for the other to handle paying that bill.

The purpose of sharing financial obligations is to take as much stress out of money in your marriage as possible. Both parties are more apt to become impatient and make outbursts, because of the combination of stress that comes from living on an inadequate income. It is important that mates support each other emotionally during financially difficult times. Diggs and Paster write, *"When there isn't enough money, the man starts losing confidence in the marriage.* History has shown us that he frequently has walked away as the last vestige of personal control and out of sadness for his inability to provide. When two people truly love each other, this is the ultimate tragedy."

Parrott III and Parrots agree that you should, "Encourage your mate during difficult times. It is important to go through suffering together. When you express your need for another person, that person feels valued and worthwhile. Give your mate freedom to fail. If your partner is terrified of failure, self-esteem is sure to be the culprit. Let him or her know that it is okay to be human. It's okay to make mistakes. Help your mate keep life manageable. When you are constantly overextended, always reacting to crises, it is stressful and very difficult to enjoy peace and contentment" (p.62).

Chapter Six
Spiritual Guidance

Chapter Six

Spiritual Guidance

Evans confirms that it is hard to build a solid marriage on the unstable expectations of the world. We must, however, learn to build our marriages on God's Word. Jesus told us clearly what to expect if we choose to build our lives upon the unchanging foundation of His Word.

Therefore everyone who hears these words of mine and puts them into practice is like a wise man who built his house on the rock.
The rain came down, the streams rose, and the winds blew and beat against that house; yet it did not fall, because it had its foundation on the rock.
But everyone who hears these words of mine and does not put them into practice is like a foolish man who built his house on sand.
The rain came down, the streams rose, and the winds blew and beat against that house, and it fell with a great crash.
Matthew 7:24-27

How to Have a Happy Marriage

If we dedicate our lives to following God's plan for marriage and do it according to the word, couples can experience the joy, happiness, and fulfillment that they desire. The Word of God provides stability through the changes and challenges we face in life. The world is having difficulty with marriage because they have rejected God's word and guidance on how the husband and wife should love and care for one another. If you want a successful marriage, put God in it. His Word is a solid foundation and it never changes.

Parrott III and Parrot illustrate that the Bible is filled with wisdom and knowledge on marriage. It is a key source of valuable guidance and instruction in practical terms. A principle that every wise person understands is prayer. Prayer can be defined as "a wish turned to God." God has chosen you to be the representative to the person you love. This is not a position to be taken lightly, and more importantly do not give up. Persist in prayer.

Listed are scriptures to reveal helpful assistance on marriage. I pray that you find comfort and a new realm of spirituality through these scriptures.

So they are no longer two, but one. Therefore what God has joined together, let man not separate.
Mark 10:8-9

A gentle answer turns away wrath, but a harsh word stirs up anger.
Proverbs 15:1

How to Have a Happy Marriage

Husbands love your wives and do not be harsh with them.

Colossians 3:19

A wife of noble character is her husband's crown, but a disgraceful wife is like decay in his bones.

Proverbs 12:4

Pleasant words are a honeycomb, sweet to the soul and healing to the bones.

Proverbs 16:24

But at the beginning of creation God made them male and female.

Mark 10:6

A word aptly spoken is like apples of gold in settings of silver.

Proverbs 25:11

Husbands love your wives, just as Christ loved the church and gave Himself up for her to make her holy.

Ephesians 5:25-26

He who answers before listening—that is his folly and shame.

Proverbs 18:13

Do not be yoked together with unbelievers. For what do righteousness and wickedness have in common? Or what fellowship can light have with darkness?

2 Corinthians 6:14

This scripture tell us that we will become like those whom we hang around with.

Starting a quarrel is like breaching a dam; so drop the matter before a dispute breaks out.

Proverbs 17:14

The wife's body does not belong to her alone but also to her husband. In the same way, the husband's body does not belong to him alone but also to his wife.

1 Corinthians 7:4

As charcoal to embers and as wood to fire, so is a quarrelsome man for kindling strife.

Proverbs 26:21

Love does not delight in evil but rejoices with the truth. It always protects, always trusts, always hopes, and always perseveres.

1 Corinthians 13:6-7

All should honor marriage, and the marriage bed kept pure, for God will judge the adulterer and all the sexually immoral.

Hebrews 13:4

Husbands ought to love their wives as their own bodies. He who loves his wife loves himself.
Ephesians 5:28

A quarrelsome wife is like constant dripping.
Proverbs 19:13

In the same way, their wives are to be women worthy of respect, not malicious talkers but temperate and trust worthy in everything.
1 Timothy 3:11

Better a dry crust with peace and quiet than a house full of feasting, with strife.
Proverbs 17:1

Husbands, in the same way be considerate as you live with your wives, and treat them with respect as the weaker partner and as heirs with you of the gracious gift of life, so that nothing will hinder your prayers.
1 Peter 3:7

Charm is deceptive, and beauty is fleeting; but a woman who fears the LORD is to be praised.
Proverbs 31:30

For this reason a man will leave his father and mother and be united to his wife, and the two will become one flesh.
Mark 10:7-8

A cheerful look brings joy to the heart, and good news gives health to the bones.
Proverbs 15:30

A gift given in secret soothes anger.
Proverbs 21:14

Christian husbands should be the first to honor and respect their wives. When referenced, scripture by the word head of household, it does not give the husband the authority to being the first in line, or the first to be catered to. It is not being the boss or the ruler. It means being the first to honor, the first to nurture, the first to meet your partner's needs. Leadership is important and regardless of how passive or dominant a woman is, she desires to be properly led in all aspects of the marriage. This is not an invitation for the man to dominate, but to show leadership and righteousness. A woman feels complete and secure in a marriage when the husband leads in the spiritual life as well as in the natural. A woman desires that the husband places structure in the home by taking care of the finances, discipline and training the children, and in every other area. When a husband does not exercise such leadership, a wife becomes frustrated. Lack of "headship" is one of the most common complaints in marriages. Headship in this sense means the husband is to be the leader in righteousness, godliness and holiness. He is to be an example of what is right and good. Ephesians 5:23, says the husband is to be the head *even as Christ is the head of the church.* If a man does take on his role and lead, the woman dominates, even though the Bible clearly states that, "your desire will be for your husband, and he will rule over you". Genesis 3:16

"When I counsel with a woman who dominates her home and/or who is embittered about her husband's lack of leadership, I almost always am dealing with a woman strongly influenced by fear. Whether it is fear of financial failure, fear of loneliness, or fear of personal harm; fear is of the main motivations of a dominant woman.

She wants her husband to be in control, but she fears what will happen if he takes control; therefore, she either stays in control and dominates her husband or constantly interrupts his authority, 1 John chapter 4, verse 18, says: *there is no fear in love: but perfect love casteth out fear*: The stronger the love, the less the fear. 1 Peter chapter 3, verse 5 says*: For after this manner in the old time the holy women also who trusted in God."* For women in this situation, the answer is for them to stop giving place to fear in their lives by keeping their eyes on Jesus and allowing their husbands to fail. I know of a woman who began her marriage by allowing her husband to fail. She committed to love him no matter what he did and to allow God to correct him.

This couple has now been married more than thirty years, and they are still madly in love. After failing in almost every way, her husband is now a success in almost every way. The reasons are these:

1. He did not have to constantly battle with his wife for the authority of the home. She gave it to him.

How to Have a Happy Marriage

2. He did not have to worry about failing. She loved and supported him anyway.
3. He grew to love and respect her for her faithfulness in supporting him through good times and bad. Therefore, he desired to please her.
4. She trusted God to be big enough to correct her husband, and God did.
5. She constantly crucified her desire to sin and resisted a demonic spirit of fear with the Word of God. Therefore, God's power worked through her so that she could love her husband and respect him, as she knew she should.

Do not allow fear to control your life. Fear is anti-faith, anti-love, and anti-peace. Submit yourself to God. Resist the devil, and he will flee from you (James 4:7). Not only that, your marriage will prosper greatly as you put faith in God and His Word" (Evans, 1994, p. 147,148).

The husband may resent the wife's expectations of leadership, but you must remember that God has given you this authority to lead and will give you the ability to lead. Husband, pray and seek God about issues in your home and how to make major decisions and how to be head of the household. A wife loves it when her husband is responsible, it removes the burdens from her and she is more willing to express love.

God wants men to be caring authorities, not dominating through carnal authority. When a man becomes controlling and dominating it makes him an oppressor.

Husband, don't allow yourself to be mislead by the misguided notions of society on what a real man is. It is not in the image of having total control or being the "super macho-man". The answer is in God's plan, the Biblical standards of love and order.

The word "Submit", it means lower yourself to those that are worthy of respect. However, It means to affirm that others are valued and important enough to be heard and love. As Ephesians chapter 5, verse 21 says: "*Submit to one another out of reverence for Christ.*" That's the key principle. It means deny "self", get rid of pleasing ourselves and once that is accomplished then you can work towards becoming one in marriage. All of us are called to submit. Not only wives to husbands, but husbands to wives also. The Bible does not say for the husband to make his wife submit. The Bible does not give the husband a command to dictate as ruler over his wife but to give up his desire to be master. Many women have fear and reservations of submitting to their husbands in a Biblical way, because they do not want to be taken advantage of, or dominated by a selfish man who will exploit them. When a husband or wife is loving each other with understanding, gentleness, warmth, and communication, it is relatively easy for them to submit to each other. Submission is equally important; husbands are to submit to their wives and wives to their husbands

Nevertheless, stop the vicious cycle of unmet needs and focus on victory and blessings. Once again, when a man and a woman fulfill their respective roles God's way, each will be protected. When you do your part, it makes it easier and safe for your spouse to do his or her part. The changes may not occur over night but have faith in God and persevere. God will reward you.

Couples should work on finding and building their spiritual practices. One way to achieve this is by praying together, and attending worship, keeping God as first in your life. Prayer is extremely important. Make time to pray together a priority.

Even though our walk with the Lord is on an individual basis, we can strengthen our marriage through working together for the Lord. It is important that spouses encourage each other spiritually. The spiritual aspect of a healthy marriage is most important and most rewarding, but the least talked about. It has been reported that spiritual marriages have a strong and positive connection between religion and marital harmony, but only if the couples make religion their priority and ultimate goal.

Couples, who are willing to allow God's word to guide their marriage, hold the key to a healthier, happier, longer marriage. The spiritual component is the most important element of a successful marriage. The Bible clearly states that they that are led of the Spirit are the sons of God. When we are led of the Spirit, we no longer lean to our own understanding. Aligning your feelings and responses to your mate's with what the scriptures say has tremendous advantages. Do so, in spite of how you think a situation should be. The Lord said that his thoughts are not our thoughts, neither are our ways his ways. For as the heavens are higher than the earth, so are my thoughts than your thoughts. Once we learn to take confidence and faith in God's word, it is then that we can experience the best possible results and happiness in our marriages.

One must forget about the traditions and what we have learned according to man and recognize that man has failed in marriage and in the way of life. There are times in marriage when one may feel discouraged, disconcerted and want to give up and ask what is the purpose for trying? But, turn to the word of God, not knowing how things are going to work out. Believe and trust in the awesome power of God. Remember what David said in Psalms 119; verse 105; *"Thy word is a lamp unto my feet and a light unto my path. "* When there seems to be no hope, no way out, perplexed in our minds; God is there to lead us in our darkest hour and most distressed times.

If a man can acknowledge his weaknesses and shortcomings, it puts him a position for God to help him, save him from self-destruction and put him on a path to righteousness and victory. However, for many men, acknowledging their need for help is not easy. Often men are hindered by their pride. Often because an individual refuses to seek help, when trouble arises in their marriage, the lack of knowledge destroys a home. Typically one mate begins to loose the love that once was. Recognize that all it takes is yielding to God's word for guidance and direction to make a home happy and complete.

Chapter Seven

Trust/Honesty/Expectations

Chapter Seven

Trust/Honesty/Expectations

Unquestioned trust is the bridge that carries marriage from a feeling of insecurity to the comfort of knowing that you are loved and are made to feel secure. In every marriage there are sets of expectations of each other. In a marriage it is important not to confuse expectations with demands. A demand implies control and causes friction. For example, if a wife expects for her husband to respond in a certain way (the way that she prefers) or to do things in a particular fashion (the way she thinks is right) that would feel more like a demand not an expectation. This type of expectation will end up in a head-on confrontation.

Because we have expectations, when we say marriage, the trust, honesty, security comes to mind. Marriage means, a person is trusted to be faithful, trusted to not harm, reject, or control each other. Trust that you will keep each other and your marriage as a top priority, and trust that you love each other

How to Have a Happy Marriage

without ulterior motives. We want to feel secure and trust in the thought that our spouse will not abandon us in the face of conflict, anger, or disagreements. In a marriage we must trust that our mate is trustworthy. When unquestioned trust is established between spouses, it serves as a reminder that your marriage is a reflection of your true spirituality. If a marriage does not have unquestioned trust the bases of the marriage are unstable.

Once trust is damaged, it causes tremendous emotional and spiritual distance in relationships. Trust is not easily reestablished. Parrott III and Parrott report, ***"One of my biggest fears is that my husband will have an affair. I have no objective grounds to suspect this, and I don't think I'm paranoid, but it's just that there are so many stories of this happening to couples. What can we do to protect our marriage against extramarital affairs?"***

People enter into extramarital relationships for a variety of reasons. Sometimes they are motivated by excitement or variety. Some are motivated by desire to "prove" to themselves that they are desirable to the opposite sex. In other cases, people may be dissatisfied with their marriage and use an affair to hurt their spouse. In such instances the offending party may be quite indiscreet to ensure that the "wronged" spouse will discover the infidelity. Whatever the reasons for affairs, every couple must consider themselves at risk to some degree or another.

Proverbs chapter 6:, verses 27-28 says: *"Can a man take fire in his bosom, and his clothes not be*

How to Have a Happy Marriage

burned? Can one go upon hot coals and his feet not be burned?

It is difficult to estimate the prevalence of extramarital affairs, but some surveys have reported that about half of all married men and a quarter of married women admitted to extramarital sexual intercourse at least once by age forty.1 Experts see few signs that this disturbing trend will diminish.

What can couples do to protect their marriage against the irreversible damage of infidelity? Christian counselor and author of **Broken Promises**, Henry Virkler believes that a first step is becoming aware of several common myths couples carry about affairs.2 Such beliefs, often held by Christians, are:

1. *The majority of affairs start because of lust.* The truth is that most affairs, especially for women, occur because of unmet emotional needs for friendship and security.

2. *A strong personal faith in Christ inoculates a person against an affair.* A personal faith may reduce to some degree the likelihood of an affair, but the inoculation is far from one hundred percent effective.

3. *We don't really need to worry about an affair in our marriage because they rarely happen in good marriages.* Again, a good marriage may reduce the chances of an affair, but it cannot be taken for granted.

4. *A man having an affair will almost always choose a lover who is physically more attractive than his wife.* This false belief is

How to Have a Happy Marriage

connected to the idea that sex is the most important ingredient in an affair.

5. *When a spouse's affair is discovered, it is best for the offended party to pretend not to know, and thereby avoid a crisis.* This approach is often taken out of fear of the consequences, but if the behavior is not confronted, it very likely will be repeated again and again.

After facing up to these common misbeliefs, a couple can further protect their marriage against an affair by identifying the kinds of situations in which each is the most vulnerable and come up with a plan to avoid such circumstances. For example, maybe going to a business lunch with a person of the opposite sex is not a good idea. In such cases, you could always be sure to include another associate, bring up your affection for your spouse in the conversation, and so on. The idea is to plan beforehand ways of avoiding circumstances that hold the slightest possibility for infidelity. Without a conscious intention, some behavior can unintentionally draw two people into an affair.

Couples should always remember that making love is one of the ways you communicate your deepest feelings of love. It is precious, something that you trust that your partner will cherish and protect. Avoid the trauma of infidelity in your marriage.

If trust has been betrayed in your marriage, take responsibility of your own trustworthiness, which does not depend on your partner's behavior. Uphold the commitment of marriage.

How to Have a Happy Marriage

If your partner broke the trust in your marriage by having an affair, you should continue to show your trustworthiness by not committing the same act. If your partner speaks harshly or acts abusively, you do not retaliate by doing the same. If your partner threatens to leave, you do not come up with threats as well. You make sure that you do not engage in a "tit-for-tat" game. If you really value being trustworthy you begin by valuing it in yourself.

Couples should not damage trust in their marriage by getting caught up in fears and desires. When trust has been damaged, do not blame your partner, or focus on their shortcomings. You cannot expect your partner to come through with unquestioned trust but do not hold yourself to the same standard. Trust is one of the strongest bonds in marriage.

One important note is that whenever a couple is experiencing growth change, such as the birth of a child, starting a new job, more than usual instability is created in their lives. It is of the utmost importance to stay close emotionally as well as physically. It is during these difficult transitional periods couples let their guard down and make themselves vulnerable to temptation.

Chapter 8

Quality Time

Chapter 8

Quality Time

Husbands and wives must make time and plans for getaways. Take the initiative to plan quiet time or a weekend away from the kids and all other social activities. Get away frequently so that you do not lose touch with your mate. Time alone rekindles love and friendship in a marriage. Show affection for your spouse during this alone time. Hold hands. Couples should acknowledge the good qualities in their mates and express their appreciation. Spending quality time reduces the risk of losing that loving feeling and becoming bored. Do not get stuck in a rut; together try something new and exciting. Be spontaneous. These are loving gestures that help to maintain a marriage because they acknowledge the importance of your relationship. Speak the truth sweetly to each other, cuddle, and take the time to express kindness. These affectionate gestures are not easy to accomplish when couples are entangled in their day-to-day schedules.

Married couples need time to bond and relate properly; they need time and energy for one another every day. Don't sacrifice your marriage for family and friends. You and your spouse need time to be together and work on your marriage.

When two people love one another as Paul described in Ephesians 5, the result is deepened love, intimacy, and trust. Practicing marriage according to God's blueprint and the Biblical role promotes growth in a relationship year after year. When you don't think it can get any better, it does. Sometimes you have to pinch yourself to see if your marriage is real. Your feelings and emotions are so fulfilled, you are so happy and respect is deep. Your yearnings and desires are so strong. The relationship will continue to get better, so long as you fulfill your Biblical responsibilities. The opposite transpires when you do not follow God's plan for marriage. The marriage begins to deteriorate and hopes and dreams are turned into a nightmare.

Marriage requires reprioritizing our relationships. We can no longer occupy or be the priority on our lists. Our spouses are to become top priority and first. We must separate from our parents and in-laws and spend not only quality time, but also quantity time with our spouses, so that a strong bond is built and separate identities are established.

Chapter Nine

In-Laws/Extended Family and Friends

Chapter Nine

In-Laws/Extended Family and Friends

While we all need other relationships in our lives, if unrestrained, when relationships are not prioritized they can cause problems in a marriage. Almost all married couples have problems with their in-laws; however, while in-laws may be a part of them, they can also lighten the load. Some couples are happy about their in-laws, while other couples feel that their in-laws are the main source of most of their problems in their marriage. In-laws, friends, parents, too much time on the telephone, anything or anyone that takes time and energy away from your spouse poses a real threat to the marriage.

Many married couples get confused in their relationships with parents or in-laws because they are unable to make the distinction between authority and respect. Couples should not allow friends and family to interfere in their marriage. Friends and family can cause unnecessary havoc, especially if one is living in the same household. The Bible says, "Let a man leave his father and mother and cleave to his wife" (Genesis 2:24-25). Evans (1994), confirms that those verses are God's definitive words setting the foundational laws of marriage. After God commanded us to leave (relinquish/loosen the bonds) our parents, thereby sets a standard for proper priorities in marriage. God commands the husband to zealously pursue her and energetically cling to her for the rest of his life. From the very beginning, God has known the secret of staying in love and that secret is work! Marriage only works when you work at it.

Staying married, happily, is what counts most in life. Keeping a strong spiritual connection with God, joined with the joys and happiness of a successful marriage is living the ultimate life. Life becomes easier, and you become secure with being yourself.

When building your marriage and you are faced with difficult time, in your marriage, it is not wise to turn to family members or friends that can not give you positive support. Everyone requires some type of emotional and practical support when under fire. If you do not have someone to talk with and pray with concerning your marriage difficulties, find a good pastor and godly friends who will give you the support that you need.

The best place to look for positive support is within a Bible-believing church or community. Look for a pastor, counselor, support group, and/or a godly individual to whom you can talk and with whom you can pray regularly concerning your situation.

How to Have a Happy Marriage

Be sure the counsel given you is Biblical. You don't need a lot of opinion. You need godly counsel and encouragement.

In seeking such encouragement, carefully consider this advice: Be careful with whom you share the details of your life and marriage. It is especially tempting for women to tell intimate details to family members and friends. Unless they are very mature and godly people, you are making a mistake. If you go to more than two or three people with your problems, you could very well be making a mistake.

Seek godly, mature people and share with them your problems and feelings. Pray together and as you pray with them and talk to them, ask them to pray for you regularly and keep you accountable by honest confrontation and advice.

Don't be discouraged or influenced by unrighteous people who encourage you to the wrong thing or persecute you for doing the right thing. Follow God and seek the encouragement you need from people who are godly. If you do this, you will be able to withstand the vast amount of ungodly advice and influence from people in the world. You will find it difficult to withstand the pressure to sin if you do not seek God and encouragement from Godly people. 10

Chapter Ten

Intimacy

Chapter Ten

Intimacy

God designed sexual intimacy for both pleasure and procreation of the human race. Sex is intended to be an expression of love, not lust. We live in such a world where sex has been exploited and is a sinful weakness. We must take the time to be informed and careful as to how one seeks to fulfill this important area of marriage.

God who created this delight in the first place, wanted us to have pleasure. God intended that man and woman share a deep personal area of their lives that creates a special bond as it produces closeness and mutual satisfaction. God created sex for intimacy, and mutual satisfaction; however, as per usual, everything else God has created, Satan has done everything he can to prevent it and use it to destroy us.

Once again if we would allow God's word to guide us even in his aspect of our lives, the word can teach us how to fulfill our needs for sex while avoiding the pitfalls of destruction. There are areas

How to Have a Happy Marriage

of sexual involvement that are clearly outlawed according to the comments of God.

1. Sex outside of marriage: adultery, fornication.
2. Sex relations with a member of the same sex: homosexuality.
3. Sex relations with a member of your family: incest.
4. Sex relations with animals: bestiality
5. Sex fantasies or desires for someone other than your spouse, which amounts

to adultery in God's sight: pornography of any kind, as well as mentally

playing out lustful desires for real or imaginary women or men.

6. Sex that finds pleasure in pain or violence: rape, sadomasochism, and brutality.
7. Sex that involves body parts not designed by God for intercourse: sodomy, anal sex.

There are parameters God has placed on sex, but we are free to enjoy safe sex with one another. God is not a prude, and sex is not "dirty." God has commanded that we do not perform certain sex acts because He knows destruction waits. Therefore, when we learn to trust and accept the restrictions He has placed on our sexual practices, we can enjoy invigorating sex and fulfillment in marriage.

When teaching marriage classes many questions often arise about sex acts that are not specifically forbidden in Scripture and that the Bible does not address. In order to address these questions, one

How to Have a Happy Marriage

must stop and ask themselves questions with God in mind. Ask is the activity hygienically and physically safe? Can I do this with a clear conscience before God? (God is not a prude, He created sex.) Also, continue to pray about it or simply decide not do it. Most importantly, you must be able to have a clear conscience before God.

Whether we as men like to admit it or not, the truth of the matter is often times because of ignorance in the area of a woman's sexual makeup, many problems are created. The reason is that many men think women basically are just like men. Therefore, they want their wives to be turned on by looking at their naked bodies. They expect their wives to turn on and off as quickly as they do.

Also, they want their wives to have "mountaintop" experiences every time they make love. Sorry! Those expectations will not happen, because women are very different from men as it relates to sex.

Consider this list from an article published in a national magazine about "sex secrets women wish husbands knew"

1. Great sex, for a woman, begins with her life as a whole.
2. Many women find talk a "turn-on."
3. Women, too, have performance anxiety.
4. Attention after sex can be vital to a woman's satisfaction.
5. Women need non-sexual touching and tenderness.

How to Have a Happy Marriage

Those "sex secrets" normally leave men cold, because they want women's sex secrets to be something like this:

1. Blow in my ear at a 45-degree angle.
2. Unbutton your shirt slowly, as I gaze upon your sculptured body.
3. Grab me passionately and throw me around the bed.
4. Stroke my body wildly with your rough, unclean hands.
5. Give me no notice of your interest in sex. I love it when you come home from work, ignore me all evening, then take me passionately right before you go to sleep.

Physically and emotionally, women respond to sex much differently than men. One person expressed the differences like this: "In the world of sex, men are microwave ovens, and women are crock pots." In other words, women cannot separate what happened this morning before breakfast from sex this evening. Everything in her life is a part of her sexual makeup. Men are completely different. After having a terrible day and knowing Armageddon is starting tomorrow morning, they can still think about sex. Although men are that way, they must understand and respect the differences in their wives. When we do this our wives will be much more sexually responsive.

A man should care for his wife and love her in non-sexual ways all day long, by complimenting her on her beauty, or commending her for being such a

126

wonderful wife and friend. Women should also be aware of the needs of their husbands. Women are also unaware of how a man is designed sexually. Whereas women are romantic and emotional by nature, men are visual and physical. So just as a man should meet his wife's need for love and romance, a woman should meet her husband's visual and physical needs. A wife needs to reveal her body to her husband and to allow full, satisfying body contact as a part of sex.

Because men typically have a stronger need for sex than women, sex is not just a preference or a pleasant event. It is a major need in his life. When a woman understands this truth, it is much easier for her to meet this need in her husband. As she does so in an aggressive and creative manner, she will be giving a great blessing to her husband and to their relationship. Two areas that affect the level of sexual enjoyment that many women experience include: 1) previous sexual and/ or physical abuse; and, 2) guilt. It is common to hear stories of sexual abuse by fathers, grandfathers, brothers, cousins, neighbors, and strangers. Every story of abuse is tragic, and most are almost unbelievable.

When women have been sexually abused, they react in different ways. Some women feel dirty and guilty, so they begin a life of sexual promiscuity to deal with their inner feelings. Other women become frigid and sexually unresponsive, unable to disassociate their past tragedy with the overall subject of sex. For them, sex is a constant reminder of ugly scars in their lives.

How to Have a Happy Marriage

Still other women block the memories of awful abuse out of their minds, refusing to deal with pain from the past. However, while their thoughts and feelings about sex may not be active in their conscious minds, past abuse prevents their functioning normally in the present.

Regardless of how a woman or man reacts to sexual abuse, eventually it must be faced and dealt with. In order to fulfill the demands of a marriage and to engage in a progressively successful intimate relationship, past experiences affect our current relationships. God created sex as a pleasurable and joyful experience between husband and wife, it is not an act to be ashamed of nor should it cause a feeling of disgust or be viewed as a chore. Intimacy is designed as a time for bonding and developing closeness.

Chapter Eleven

Identifying Strengths and Weaknesses

Chapter Eleven

Identifying Strengths and Weaknesses

The inability to openly express feelings, also known as secrets, is commonly characteristic of troubled marriages. Yet many couples fail to recognize areas of distress in their relationship. It is important to be able to identify, and know how to cope with problem areas within your relationship.

Determining ways to help couples effectively cope and maintain healthy and happy marriages is the purpose of this project. This chapter discusses data collection and analysis to establish one of the objectives of this study, and presents a summary of the results of the data analysis pertaining to strength and weaknesses of marriage, as well as surveys as instrumental tools to identify problem areas in marriages. During a marriage class the researcher conducted, twenty questionnaires were distributed to couples. The participants were asked to respond to fifteen

Likert-style statements. The participants had a choice of five responses. Strongly Disagree (1); Disagree (2); Neutral (3); Agree (4);or Strongly Agree (5). The participants were asked to answer each question according to their current experiences and to answer as candidly as they could. They were informed that the answers would be kept completely confidential and are being used for research purposes only.

In order to improve a troubled relationship, the problem must first be identified. Whether the problem is communication, listening, conflict resolution or problem solving, the issue remains a problem until it is labeled for what it really is, "a problem". In this instance, the survey conducted was geared toward identifying strengths, weaknesses and vulnerabilities in relationships among the couples of the surveyed population. Sometimes weaknesses are unknown, and go undetected.

This is a good example of how essential it is to educate, implement training programs and include a prep test on marriage. Develop more programs that will improve marriage and decrease the divorce rate.

When asked whether they feel that they could talk fairly easily about strong or positive feelings with their partner (Question 1), 40% of the respondents strongly agreed, 45% agreed, 5% were neutral, 5% disagreed and 5% strongly disagreed.

Statement	Strongly Disagree	Disagree	Neutral	Agree	Strongly Agree	Mean	Standard Deviation
I feel that I can talk fairly easily about strong or positive feelings with my partner (Question 1)	5%	5%	5%	45%	40%	4.1	0.23
My partner often does not listen to me when I describe my feelings (Question 3)	25%	15%	15%	40%	5%	2.85	0.3

When asked whether my partner often does not listen to me when I describe my feelings (Question 3), forty percent of the respondents agreed, 5% strongly agreed, 15% were neutral, 15% disagreed and 25% strongly disagreed. Both of these questions were related to how well couples communicate in their relationship. Based on the results, it was concluded that if 40% of the participants agreed that they were not being listened to, this response could be identified as a weakness in communication and listening skills in the marriage. See chapter one for effective coping tools.

There was also a contrast in the responses, most of the couples felt that they could speak openly and freely to their spouses, yet the majority of the respondents felt that they were not being listened to by their spouse.

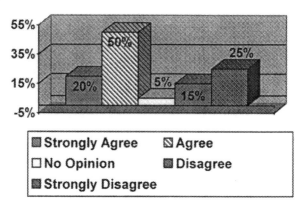

When asked whether they have differences in opinions about how to solve a given problem and seldom find a compromise, fifty percent of the respondents agreed, 35% strongly agreed, 10% were neutral, 10% disagreed and none strongly disagreed. These results clearly identify a weakness in problem-solving and conflict resolution.

When couples were asked whether they share the financial obligations in their household, sixty percent of the respondents agreed, 15% strongly agreed, 10% were neutral, and none strongly disagreed. This question focused on problem solving.

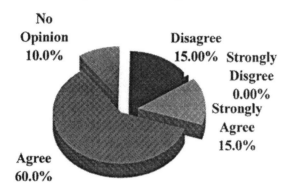

Based on the results of the data analysis, the couples were practicing effective problem solving skills when dealing with issues of finances and household obligations. In this example, "problem solving" is a strength.

Finally, when the population was asked when they have sexual relations, do they have orgasm at least half of the time and so does their partner, sixty percent of the respondents agreed, 15% strongly agreed, 15% were neutral, 5% disagreed and 5% strongly disagreed. For the respondents that agreed, this would be an area of strength and just the opposite for those that disagreed. This served as an opportunity for couples to identify the problem, and then proceed to find an effective coping strategy to decrease distress in their marriage.

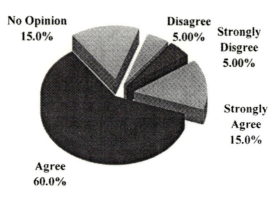

Interpersonal Contact

Purpose:
Certain elements comprise what we call interpersonal contact. By completing this survey, couples can rate their ability to make contact and then discuss differences in their assessment.

Task I:
Read the following items and respond in terms of how often these statements are true for you. Please be sure to rate all items.

        5 = All the time
        4 = Most of the time
        3 = More often than not

How to Have a Happy Marriage

2 = Occasionally
1 = Rarely
0 = Never

(Each partner circles with different color or one partner circles and the other places a square around the number.)

1. My spouse and I stay focused on what we need to resolve.

   5   4   3   2   1   0

2. When I am angry with my spouse. I express it.

   5   4   3   2   1   0

3. I know what I like and what I don't like.

   5   4   3   2   1   0

4. When we go out, it doesn't matter to me how my spouse looks.

   5   4   3   2   1   0

5. I give up my way of doing something if my spouse strongly objects.

   5   4   3   2   1   0

6. There is nothing to be settled or worked on in my marriage.

   5   4   3   2   1   0

How to Have a Happy Marriage

7. My spouse and I   5   4   3   2   1   0
   communicate in ways
   in addition to talking.

8. I have well-defined set   5   4   3   2   1   0
   of values and beliefs.

9. My spouse and I move   5   4   3   2   1   0
   through our fixed and
   standard schedule.

How to Have a Happy Marriage

Interaction (Continued)

Interpersonal contact occurs between people at a point, which draws their common interest or experience. This interest is called common figure. These attempts to assess how able partners are to choose common topics to discuss, engage in common interests and share time together.

Discussion

1. Compare your scores. Where are your strengths and what do you need to work on?

2. How are you different in terms of your likes and dislikes, values and beliefs?

3. Are these differences respected in your relationship?

4. Do you negotiate your differences well?

How to Have a Happy Marriage

5. Are you open to being influenced and to try new things?

6. Is there give and take and do you share your deepest feelings?

7. Can you stay on topic until it is resolved?

8. What is the common ground between you? What mutual values, interests, etc. do you share?

9. Can you freely express anger, affection, fear, or sadness?

10. Is touch permitted and freely given?

Space and Time Boundaries

Purpose:

It is important to find our whether you and your partner are satisfied with time and space management in the relationship. As children, some of us had little or no private space. Some of us were told that our rooms or belongings were private, only to find that such spaces were invaded regularly with little or no regard for how we felt. As adults, violations of space may seem perfectly natural to one partner but be absolutely unacceptable to the other partner. It is important for each to determine and express spatial needs so that clear boundaries can be set and honored. Lines need to be drawn so that both partners have space to call their own.

Time is another important issue (see chapter 8). Many adults had homes where they had either too much or too little alone time. Some families had unbending rules around time. Everyone sat down to dinner every night at a certain hour. Others had few requirements: members fixed their own plates and ate in front of the T.V. Partners need to discuss the importance of both alone and together time, and encourage one another to share feelings so that they can reach a healthy balance in the relationship.

How to Have a Happy Marriage

Task:

Answer the following questions and discuss these answers with your partner.

1. What space(s) in your home is personal which no one else uses (e.g. study, desk area, favorite chair, separate bedroom)?

2. What time do you prefer to spend alone? Do you let your partner know when you need alone time?

3. When does your whole family spend time together?

4. What kinds of activities do you do with your entire family? (For example, do you go to church together as a family? Do you eat certain meals together?

5. Do you and your spouse set-aside times to spend together alone? When? How often?

6. If you have children, does each of you spend individual time with each of your children?

How to Have a Happy Marriage

7. How much time and emotional energy do you invest in your children's activities?

8. Do you have separate friends with whom you socialize without your partner being present? How often? Do you ever feel jealous or left out when your partner is with his or her friends?

9. Do you invite people into your home? Is there agreement about when and how often this should happen?

10. Do people visit your home uninvited? How often does this happen? How does each of you feel about this?

As humorous and as basic as the above questions and interaction may appear, there are issues that exist that surface in relationships and can cause turmoil and anguish. Often these issues are silent offenders that hinder growth and healthy relationships. If only we would take the time to get to know the needs of our partners and how to go about getting our needs met.

To establish a successful relationship, partners must acquire the ability to open their senses to see and hear and ask for what they want. Each of the surveys were chosen to help reach beyond the surface of your

How to Have a Happy Marriage

relationship and to break unhealthy patterns and to risk sharing vulnerability, a necessary component to establish trust and intimacy.

Conclusion

Marriage has the power to make people miserable or ecstatic. Therefore it is important to be well informed and to make adequate preparation before marriage. Marriage is a complex institution of spiritual, physical, financial, social, domestic, and mental requirements. It is more than just sex, and birthing beautiful children. Sex and producing children are only two of the many obvious and pleasurable aspects of marriage.

A good marriage is like a good diamond, most of the time you have to remove the diamond from the rough to get to the beauty. Marriage is to be taken seriously. Keep it a top priority so that you hold on to your interest in the marriage and excitement for one another. Openly express your love, care and concern for your companion. When you make your marriage a top priority, being together enhances all other events and situations. Keep your heart-to-heart connection with a special look, a touch, or with a spoken" I love you".

How to Have a Happy Marriage

Many people have the misconception that if they find the right person, they will be happy all of the time. It is because of this misguided notion that many people have made a mistake when they face problems in their marriage. They are willing to give up on that they have invested into the relationship and to go back out into the world and try to find "the right one" again. This is not the answer. Every marriage is going to experience problems. No married couple will have all good days and affirmative feelings about one another all of the time. You don't want a soap opera, romance-novel mentality relationship. You should want a committed hard-working relationship where you do what is right and have faith in God that He will supply the proper results. You can't be proud or lazy - this will lead to a failed marriage. Instead, be productive and willing to learn.

Jesus suffered for your sin when you were out in the world. It if was not for His righteous suffering, the world would be in a hopeless mess today. But because of Jesus' unadulterated, sacrificial love, we have a means of deliverance and restoration.

Remember each of you must have a willingness to suffer. While suffering is not pleasant, suffering is inevitable. Sometimes, in life and marriage, we will suffer. Not meaninglessly or unnecessarily long-drawn-out suffering; but in order to learn how to endure, build and grow, suffering is inevitable.

In the book of 1 Peter we are instructed to endure times of suffering. But how is it to your credit if you receive a beating for doing wrong and endure it? But if you suffer for doing good and you endure it, this is commendable before God.

The greatest pathway to success and pleasure in marriage is having knowledge of God's word, Hosea chapter 4; verse 6 says: *My people are destroyed for a lack of knowledge.* The word of God provides us with all that we need to guide us pertaining to how to conduct ourselves in every aspect of life. There is great strength added to a marriage when two people refuse to give up. *Seek first His kingdom and His righteousness, and all these things will be given to you.*

Remember, a strong marriage is not produced from a fairy-tale existence. It is produced by two people committed to working and sacrificing throughout their lives to make their marriage all it can be. Do not be merely drawn into marriage. Be completely, without doubt, committed to your marriage! From this foundation, you can be assured of stability and success.

Jesus spoke of the parable of the seed that fell on thorny soil. The seed fell on unproductive soil, soft and deep enough for seed to grow, but too crowded. Rather than working to establish a good, clean environment in which to cultivate seed, the thorny-soil person lives life at random, allowing whatever comes along to attach itself either to him or around him.

As it relates to marriage, we must build the proper disciplines into our relationships and refuse to allow those influences that are harmful or unnecessary to grow up around us. For example, the discipline of a personal relationship with God is the most important ingredient to a successful marriage, but it requires

How to Have a Happy Marriage

effort to achieve it. We also must learn to pursue each other and to meet each other's needs, but this also takes discipline.

Finances, children, church involvement, keeping priorities straight, and maintaining personal health all required discipline. Whenever we work at keeping our lives healthy, the result will be lasting pleasure and success. However, when we do not discipline ourselves to build and maintain the proper balance in our lives, the result will be a deteriorating lifestyle overcome by problems undealt with. Mismanagement and a lack of discipline are a needless way to lose the satisfaction of a once-pleasurable marriage.

If you are just now getting married, work every day to build the right disciplines in your relationship. If you have been married a while and realize your love life has become choked by unhealthy attitudes and habits, repent of you error and begin today to discipline yourself properly.

Remember, the prize isn't won simply because one enjoys the sport or activity. An individual wins because he has disciplined himself to do those things that are necessary and will cause him to succeed. In the same manner, your marriage will not succeed simply because you thought it was a good idea and that worked in the beginning. It will only succeed in the long run as you build into your life the proper disciplines that lead to success.

Knowledge of God's Word, commitment to the relationship, and daily, personal discipline are three foundations essential for the protection and permanence of the blessings of God desires to bestow upon

How to Have a Happy Marriage

us in marriage. It is foolish to build a house without a foundation. It is equally foolish to expect marriages to remain permanently satisfying without the proper groundwork foundation.

God designed marriage to be a union that would produce pleasure and benefits beyond measure. He did not design these blessings to be temporary. He meant for them to grow and last for the rest of our lives. In fact, God's plan intends the blessings of marriage to grow in intensity throughout all our years of marriage. But, in order for this to happen, we must be like good soil: ready to be taught, deep in character, and disciplined for success.

More importantly, if you commit yourself to meeting the unique and special needs of your husband or wife, the love in your marriage will grow stronger and will insure faithfulness and security. You will build a marriage that will retain its romance, intimacy and closeness year after year.

That you have been enlightened and encouraged is my hope and prayer.

Footnotes

1. R. Segraves, (1989). "Effects of Psychotropic Drugs on Human Erection and Ejaculation," *Archives of General Psychiatry 46,* pp. 275-84: G. Wyatt, S. Peters and D. Guthrie Kinsey, (1988). "Comparisons of the Sexual Socialization and Sexual Behavior of White Women over 33 Years," *Archives of Sexual Behavior 17,* pp. 201-39.

2. Henry Virkler, Broken Promises, (1992). Understanding, Healing and Preventing Affairs in Christian Marriages", Dallas: Word.

3. *Democrat and Chronicle*. 2000, March.

4. Rivoli, M. L. and Bracely, M.D, 1999 February 10, "How they do "I do" Longtime wedded couples offer their insights into lasting marriage," *Democrat and Chronicle.*

5. Woolfolk, *Light Her Fire Student Workbook* (p. 56).

6. J.B. Stiff, J.L. Hale R. Garlick, and R.G. Rogan, "Effect of Cue Incongruence and Social Normative Influences on Individual Judgments"

7. Acock, C. A., (1994). *Family Diversity and Well-Being:* Sage Library of Social Research.

8. B. H. Spitzberg, (1994). "The Dark Side of Incompetence," in *The Dark Side of Interpersonal Communication*, Hillsdale, N.J.: Erlbaum, pp. 27-28.

9. Borisoff and Purdy (eds.), *Listening in Everyday Life*, p xiii.

10. Jimmy Evans, *Marriage on the Rock, God's Design For Your Dream Marriage,* pp.197, 210-211.

11. Jimmy Evans, *Marriage on the Rock, God's Design For Your Dream Marriage,* pp.259-262.

12. Jimmy Evans, *Marriage on the Rock, God's Design For Your Dream Marriage.*

13. Bunny S. Suhl, (Ed.). (1976). *The Interpersonal Vulnerability Contract.* D Boston Family Institute, Brookline, MA., pp. 29, 37, 39-41, 53-55.

Bibliography

Anita Doreen Digs and Dr. Vera S, Paster. (1988). *Staying Married: A Guide for African American Couples.*

Drs. Evelyn and Paul Moschetta , *The Marriage Spirit Finding The Passion and Joy of Soul Centered Love.*

Dr. Les Parrott III & Dr. Leslie Parrott, *Questions Couples Ask.*

Gary Smalley, *For Better or For Best.*

Dr. John Wright, *Bridges to Intimacy, Survival Strategies for Couples.*

Gary Smalley, *Secrets to Lasting Love* 646.78 s635s.

Tim & Beverly Lahaye with Mike Yorkey, *The Act of Marriage after 40.*

How to Have a Happy Marriage

Jacqueline Rickard, *Save Your Marriage Ahead of Time*.

Michael J. McManus, *Marriage Savers*, Foreword by George Gallup, Jr.

The National Data Book: Statistical Abstract of the United States, 120th Edition: 2000.

Henry James Borys, *The Way of Marriage*.

Bill & Lynne Hybels, *Fit To Be Tied*.

Acock, C. A., (1994). *Family Diversity and Well-Being:* Sage Library of Social Research.

Judith S. Wallerstein & Sandra, (1995). *The Good Marriage, How & Why Love Lasts*, Blakeslee.

About the Author

Happily married for 45 years to his beautiful wife Mattie, Oce Jones is the pastor of Christ Tabernacle Church in Rochester, New York.

Oce Jones holds a doctorate degree in Christian family and biblical counseling. His work as a spiritual leader and a marriage and family counselor creates the venue for Pastor Jones to share with others the experience, techniques and biblical principles that lead to the building of strong, lasting and successful marriages. The father of six children, Oce Jones together with his wife Mattie resides in Rochester, New York.

Inquiries regarding obtaining additional copies of this book should be forwarded to Xulon Press @ www.xulonpress.com.

How to Have a Happy Marriage

Inquiries regarding speaker availability and volume discounts for *How to Have a Happy Marriage* should be forwarded to P.O. Box 17220, Rochester, New York 14616 or to Bishopoce05@yahoo.com.

Printed in the United States
200319BV00001B/178-282/A